AQA
AS

Psychology
Revision

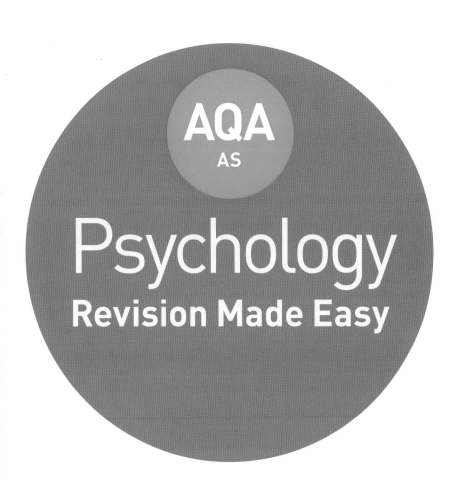

AQA
AS

Psychology
Revision Made Easy

Jean-Marc Lawton

HODDER
EDUCATION
AN HACHETTE UK COMPANY

Author's dedication: For my father – the mirror to my future.

The Publishers would like to thank the following for permission to reproduce copyright material.

Photo credits

p.2 © Kenzo Tribouillard/AFP/Getty Images; **p.4** © Christopher Dodson/iStockphoto.com; **p.6** © epa european pressphoto agency b.v./Alamy Stock Photo; **p.8** With kind permission by Philip Zimbardo, Inc.; **p.12** © Photo News Service Ltd/TopFoto; **p.14** © RTimages – Fotolia; **p.18** © EHStock/E+/Getty Images; **p.22** © HOWARD JONES/NEWZULU/PA Images; **p.28** © photogerson – Fotolia; **p.30** Map data © 2014 Google, reproduced with permission; **p.32** © Courtesy Everett Collection/REX Shutterstock; **p.36** © Tom Wang – Fotolia; **p.38** © Monkey Business – Fotolia; **p.40** © Rob – Fotolia; **p.42** © Jeffrey Phelps/Aurora Photos/Corbis; **p.44** © Monkey Business – Fotolia; **p.48** © Mike Abrahams/Alamy Stock Photo; **p.50** © imtmphoto – Fotolia; **p.54** © Simons, D. J., & Chabris, C. F. (1999). Gorillas in our midst: Sustained inattentional blindness for dynamic events. Perception, 28, 1059-1074.; **p.56** © Papirazzi – Fotolia; **p.65** © epa/Corbis; **p.67** © Howard Berman/Iconica/Getty Images; **p.70** © Everett Collection/REX Shutterstock; **p.72** © Lijuan Guo – Fotolia; **p.76** © adimas – Fotolia; **p.81** © BORACAN/SIPA/REX Shutterstock; **p.83** © AF archive/Alamy Stock Photo; **p.94** © luminastock – Fotolia; **p.101** © Antonio_Diaz/iStock/Thinkstock.

Acknowledgements

Every effort has been made to trace all copyright holders, but if any have been inadvertently overlooked, the Publishers will be pleased to make the necessary arrangements at the first opportunity.

Although every effort has been made to ensure that website addresses are correct at time of going to press, Hodder Education cannot be held responsible for the content of any website mentioned in this book. It is sometimes possible to find a relocated web page by typing in the address of the home page for a website in the URL window of your browser.

Hachette UK's policy is to use papers that are natural, renewable and recyclable products and made from wood grown in sustainable forests. The logging and manufacturing processes are expected to conform to the environmental regulations of the country of origin.

Orders: please contact Bookpoint Ltd, 130 Park Drive, Milton Park, Abingdon, Oxon OX14 4SE. Telephone: +44 (0)1235 827720. Fax: +44 (0)1235 400454. Email education@bookpoint.co.uk Lines are open from 9 a.m. to 5 p.m., Monday to Saturday, with a 24-hour message answering service. You can also order through our website: www.hoddereducation.co.uk

ISBN: 978 1 4718 4524 6

© Jean-Marc Lawton 2016

First published in 2016 by

Hodder Education,

An Hachette UK Company

Carmelite House

50 Victoria Embankment

London EC4Y 0DZ

www.hoddereducation.co.uk

Impression number   10 9 8 7 6 5 4 3 2 1

Year   2020 2019 2018 2017 2016

Cover photo © hitdelight - Fotolia

Illustrations by Aptara and Barking Dog

Typeset in India by Aptara, Inc.

Printed in Italy

A catalogue record for this title is available from the British Library.

Contents

5 Biopsychology

6 Psychopathology

7 Research methods

8 Revision and exam skills

How to use this book

This book will help you revise for your AQA AS Psychology specification (7181). It is designed so that you can use it alongside any appropriate textbook, including *AQA Psychology for A-level 1*, by Jean-Marc Lawton and Eleanor Willard. We have included page references to appropriate material in this book on each spread.

pp4 – 9

Each spread covers a different topic, outlining the headline factual knowledge you need, as well as providing evaluation material to help you aim for those top marks.

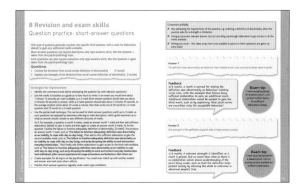

Research methods and techniques are also covered in an interesting way to help you retain and recall the information.

At the end of the book you will find guidance on making sure you are ready to tackle the exams!

1 Social influence
Types of conformity

Focal study

Asch (1955) investigated whether individuals would conform to an obviously wrong answer. 123 American male student volunteers, having been told that it was a study into visual perception, were tested in groups of between 8 and 10. The participants sat in a line or around a table. A stimulus line was presented with 3 comparison lines, 1 clearly matching the stimulus line while the other 2 did not. Participants had to say out loud which comparison line matched the stimulus. In each group there was in fact only 1 real participant, who answered either last or next to last – the other group members were all *confederates* (pseudo-participants). From 18 trials, confederates gave identical wrong answers on 12 occasions. There was a 32 per cent overall conformity rate to the wrong answers, 75 per cent conforming at least once, 25 per cent never conforming, while 5 per cent conformed all the time. It was also found that most participants conformed publicly, but not privately, a form of *compliance*, in order to avoid rejection.

OTHER STUDIES

- Mori & Arai (2010) replicated Asch's study (though using females as well as males), giving filter goggles to participants, so that one participant perceived a different comparison line to all the others. This meant *demand characteristics* (where participants attempt to guess the aim of a study and act accordingly) could not occur, unlike in Asch's study where the participant might realise the confederates were lying and so just pretended to conform. Females conformed similarly to Asch's participants, but the males a lot less. The study was unethical, as participants thought the goggles were to prevent glare.

- Bogdonoff et al. (1961) measured the stress levels encountered by participants on an Asch-type task, by recording galvanic skin responses – a measurement of electrical conductivity. High stress levels were found when participants gave true answers that went against the majority, but lower levels when individuals complied with obviously wrong answers, implying compliance to be a healthy response.

Description

Conformity occurs when a majority of people influence the beliefs and/or behaviour of a minority. There are 3 types, differing in terms of how much they affect individuals' belief systems.

1 *Compliance* involves public, but not private, agreement with a group's beliefs and behaviour, in order to gain acceptance or avoid disapproval. It is fairly temporary and weak, and only occurs within the presence of the group. For example, an individual claims allegiance to the local football team in order to fit in and be accepted, but in reality has little if any allegiance to the team.

2 *Identification* involves public and private agreement with a group's

Fig 1.1 A religious conversion would be an example of internalisation

✔ Positive evaluation

✔ Mann (1969) believed internalisation to be *true conformity*, as it is the only type of majority influence where participants are actually converted to other people's belief systems.

✔ *Internalisation* relates to *minority influence* (see **page 20**), which allows carefully considered *social change* (see **page 22**) to occur.

✔ *Compliance* allows individuals to conduct meaningful social interactions by constantly fitting in with and adapting to different groups' social norms.

✔ *Compliance* relates more to *normative social influence*, where individuals conform to fit in, while *identification* and *internalisation* relate more to *informational social influence*, as individuals genuinely agree with the behaviour they are conforming to.

beliefs and behaviour, because membership of that group is beneficial. A stronger type than compliance, it is still fairly temporary and weak, as it is not retained when an individual leaves the group. For instance, a soldier adopts the beliefs and behaviour of fellow soldiers while in the army, but adopts new beliefs and behaviour on returning to civilian life.

3 *Internalisation* involves public and private agreement and is not dependent on group membership. It is the strongest form of conformity. For instance, beliefs in a religious faith are not dependent on group members being present.

✘ Negative evaluation

✘ There are other reported reasons for why people conform in Asch's study, such as having doubts about individual perceptual ability and the accuracy of individual judgements. Therefore, it may not just be compliance that is occurring.

✘ Most studies of types of conformity, such as Asch's and Mori & Arai's, are unethical and arguably should not be performed, as they involve deceit and therefore a lack of informed consent, as well as possibly causing distress through elevating stress levels.

✘ Asch's study was time-consuming, with only 1 participant being tested at a time. As 123 participants performed 18 trials each, the experiment was conducted 2,214 times.

Practical application

Compliance helps to maintain social order, through majority influence allowing people to unthinkingly know what behaviour and attitudes are expected of them and stick to them. Internalisation meanwhile converts people's belief systems, so that social change occurs through innovative behaviours becoming accepted as mainstream.

1 Social influence
Explanations for conformity

Focal study

Jenness (1932) investigated the effect of group influence on individual judgements, by getting participants to estimate the number of jellybeans in a jar, first as individuals, then in a large group or several small groups, and finally as individuals again. It was found that participants' second individual estimates moved closer to their group estimates than their first individual estimates, with a greater effect seen among females than males. This suggests that ISI occurs in ambiguous and new situations where there is no clear correct answer. This study is more ethical than most conformity studies, as there is no deliberate deceit involved. However, like Asch's study, it was a laboratory-based experiment using an artificial and non-lifelike situation and as such lacks realism. There may also be an element of NSI, with some participants conforming due to a desire for acceptance and not just to be correct.

OTHER STUDIES

- Sherif (1935) used the *autokinetic effect*, a visual illusion, to find participants' second individual estimates – of how far a dot of light in a dark room appeared to move – converged towards a group norm after participants heard the estimates of others. This supports ISI and suggests that participants *internalised* others' judgements and made them their own.

- Bogdonoff *et al.* (1961) measured the stress levels encountered by participants on an Asch-type task, by recording galvanic skin responses – a measurement of electrical conductivity. High stress levels were found when participants gave true answers that went against the majority, but lower levels when individuals complied with obviously wrong answers, which suggests that NSI not only involves compliance, but is also a healthy thing to do.

- Eagli & Carli (1981) found in a meta-analysis of 48 studies that females conform more in public situations, suggesting that females' more nurturing, co-operative nature causes them to have a greater need for social agreement.

Description

Deutsch & Gerard (1955) suggested 2 explanations of conformity, *informational social influence* (ISI) and *normative social influence* (NSI).

Underlying ISI is a need for certainty that brings a sense of control. ISI occurs in ambiguous situations with no clear 'correct' way of behaving, as well as in novel situations not experienced before. In such situations individuals look to the majority for information on how to behave. This involves *social comparison* with others in order to reduce uncertainty. For instance, when eating in a restaurant for the first time you may look to others for which cutlery,

Fig 1.2 How many jellybeans are in the jar?

✓ As well as having research support, both NSI and ISI can be used to explain and understand real-life examples of conformist behaviour, giving them additional support as explanations.

✓ Asch initially criticised Jenness' earlier study as inferior due to having no obvious wrong answer to conform to. However, both studies are equally effective in helping to highlight explanations for conformity: ISI in Jenness' case and NSI in Asch's case.

✓ NSI and ISI should not be seen as opposing explanations; they can be combined together to give an overall explanation of conformity. Different individuals in the same situation may be conforming for reasons of NSI or ISI.

glasses etc. to use. ISI therefore involves stronger types of conformity, such as identification and internalisation, where public and private agreement with a majority occurs.

Underlying NSI is a need to belong, by being accepted and avoiding rejection and ridicule. Individuals agree with others because of their power to reward and punish – for instance, giving in to peer pressure to smoke, even though you may not wish to, in order to be accepted by the group. NSI therefore tends to involve a weaker form of conformity, compliance, where public, but not private, agreement occurs.

✗ Negative evaluation

✗ ISI can have harmful consequences in crisis situations, where negative emotions and panic can spread quickly. Jones *et al.* (2000) reported that *psychogenic* illnesses, such as mass hysteria, can occur in crisis situations through individuals having little time to think and so looking to others for cues as to how to behave.

✗ NSI can also have harmful consequences. Jordan (1996) reported that due to ridicule, punishment and rejection of non-conforming group members, 12 teenage victims of such bullying killed themselves in 1 year in Japan. NSI can also lead to destructive inter-group violence.

Practical application

To help create group cohesion (unity) in sports teams, ambiguous tasks with no correct answer/behaviour could be set, so that team members are drawn closer together through ISI.

pp. 4–9

1 Social influence
Variables affecting conformity

Focal study

Asch's variations (1956)

1 With 1 participant and 1 confederate, conformity was very low, rising to 13 per cent with 1 participant and 2 confederates, and up to 32 per cent with 1 participant and 3 confederates. Increasing confederate numbers (up to as high as 15) produced no further increases in conformity.

2 If 1 confederate sided with the real participant by giving the correct answer, conformity dropped from 32 per cent to just 5.5 per cent. More interestingly, if a confederate went against the group but gave a different wrong answer, conformity still dropped, down to 9 per cent. This suggests that the important factor is the reduction in the majority's level of agreement, rather than an individual being given support for their private opinion.

3 When task difficulty was increased, by having comparison lines more similar to each other, conformity to wrong answers increased, demonstrating the effect of task difficulty on conformity.

OTHER STUDIES

- Maslach et al. (1987) found males conform less, as they are more independent and competitive, while females conform more, as they are sensitive to others' needs and like to maintain harmony, thus explaining gender differences in conformity levels.

- Tong et al. (2008) found participants were more likely to conform to wrong answers to maths questions given by confederates when they were in a positive mood rather than in a negative or neutral one, demonstrating the effect of mood on conformity levels.

- Milgram (1961) found that Norwegians conformed more than French participants to obviously wrong answers. Avant & Knudson (1993) believe this occurs as Norway has shared cultural values, a dislike of individualism and fewer ethnic minorities with different cultural norms than France, suggesting a cultural basis for differences in conformity levels.

Description

Asch conducted variations of his study to identify *situational variables*, aspects of the environment that influence levels of conformity. These included:

- *Group size*, which showed that as a majority's size increased, so did the level of conformity, up to a maximum level, after which increases in group size did not lead to any further rise in conformity levels

- *Unanimity*, which showed that conformity rates decreased when majority influence became less unanimous, with group members dissenting against other group members' behaviour

- *Task difficulty*, which showed that greater conformity occurred when task difficulty increased, as the correct answer was less

Fig 1.3 Norwegians are conformist as they share cultural values and norms

obvious and so individuals increasingly looked to others for guidance as to the correct answer.

Research has also identified *individual variables*, characteristics of people that influence conformity levels. Important variables here include:

- *Gender*, with females conforming more, possibly due to females being socialised to be more submissive to social influence
- *Mood*, with individuals seen to conform more when in happy moods and when moving to more relaxed emotional states, possibly because they are then more amenable to majority influence
- *Culture*, with some cultures conforming more, as they possess shared values and uniformity, thus making agreement with others easier.

Practical application

Advertisers focus on the unanimity of majority influence to sell products. This relates to the 'bandwagon effect', where if individuals believe all members of a group have a product, like a certain mobile phone, then purchase of that phone will allow them to be accepted into the group.

pp. 9–12

1 Social influence

Conformity to social roles

Focal study

Zimbardo (1973) investigated the extent to which people would conform to the roles of guard and prisoner in a simulation of prison life. The participants were 21 students, who were selected for their physical and mental stability and lack of criminal history. A realistic mock prison was set up and the prisoners *dehumanised* (their individual identity was removed) by being made to wear prison uniforms and referred to by numbers instead of names. The uniformed guards' role was to keep order, though physical punishment was banned. Over the course of the experiment, the guards became increasingly abusive and most prisoners increasingly submissive. Four prisoners were released due to their poor mental state. Scheduled to run for 2 weeks, the study was stopped after 6 days when Zimbardo realised the extent of the harm that was occurring. The study illustrated that individuals conform readily to the social roles expected in a situation, even when such roles override individuals' moral beliefs.

OTHER STUDIES

- Haslam & Reicher (2002) replicated Zimbardo's study, aiming to investigate the behaviour of groups that were unequal in terms of power and status. Participants were randomly selected as guards or prisoners, with the guards constructing prison rules and punishments for breaking them. The prisoners increasingly developed a group identity, but the guards did not and were reluctant to impose authority. They were overcome by the prisoners. The participants then set up an equal social system, but this proved unsustainable and attempts to impose a harsher regime met with weak resistance, at which point the study ended. It was concluded that powerlessness and the failure of groups allows cruel domination to occur.

- Snyder (1974) found that *high self-monitors* (people who are able to respond to social cues and adjust their behaviour accordingly) were able to adapt their behaviour to fit the needs of different social situations, while the behaviour of *low self-monitors* (people who are less able to respond to social cues and adjust their behaviour accordingly) was more fixed due to innate personality traits. This suggests that some individuals are more able to conform to social roles than others.

Description

Social roles are the actions that people are expected to display in social situations. They involve the behaviours and attitudes which individuals should adopt as members of different social groups in order to fit in with, and meet the requirements of, those social situations. An individual has first to perceive what role they are expected to play within a given social situation, and then meet the expectation by 'playing the part'. Different social situations have different social roles to adopt – for example, there is an expectation that someone will be outgoing and playful at a party, but reserved and serious at a funeral. People learn social roles from

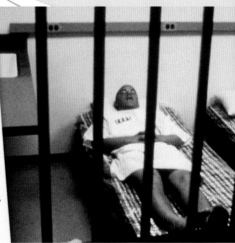

Fig 1.4 Zimbardo's study showed how people conform readily to social roles

✔ Conformity to different social roles in different social situations may have an evolutionary survival value, as it allows us to understand and adapt to the requirements of different situations and thus fit in. Social order is thereby created and maintained, permitting a safe, predictable world for individuals to interact within.

✔ Research into social roles suggests that behaviour in brutalising institutions, such as prisons, can be improved by the provision of less dehumanising environments.

✔ The fact that social roles are not permanent means people can adapt successfully to changing environments and therefore have the flexibility to meet the needs of a diverse range of social situations.

experience and they become internal mental scripts, which individuals select from in order to behave appropriately in different social settings. Conformity to social roles involves *identification* (see **page 2**), which is stronger than *compliance*, as it involves public and private acceptance of the behaviour and attitudes adopted. Conformity to social roles is not as strong as *internalisation*, which is a more permanent form of conformity, as individuals only conform to specific social roles while in particular social situations. They change their behaviour to suit new social norms when they move to new social situations.

❌ Negative evaluation

✘ Zimbardo hoped his research would lead to beneficial changes in the prison system, but he concluded that, as such, his research was a failure because if anything prison conditions have got worse.

✘ Zimbardo's study was unethical: fully informed consent was not given, there were elements of deceit, the right to withdraw was not made clear and, probably most importantly, high levels of both physical and psychological harm occurred.

✘ There seem to be large individual differences in the ability to identify and adopt required social roles. Therefore, some people are less able to successfully adapt to different environments.

Practical application
The move to all-seater football grounds following the Taylor Report (1992) saw a huge reduction in acts of hooliganism, arguably because the less brutal environments thus created led to less aggressive social roles for supporters to conform to.

pp. 13–16

1 Social influence
Obedience and the work of Milgram

Focal study

Milgram (1963) tested 40 American male volunteers, aged between 20 and 50 years, on their willingness to obey increasingly destructive orders. Believing it a study of memory and learning, volunteers drew lots with a second participant, actually a *confederate* (see **page 2**), to see who would be the 'teacher' and who the 'learner'. This was rigged; the real participant was always the teacher. The learner was strapped into a chair in an adjacent room with electrodes attached to him. It was explained by a confederate researcher wearing a laboratory coat (that gave him legitimate authority) that every time the learner got a question wrong the teacher should shock him by pressing a switch on a (fake) shock machine. If the teacher refused, the researcher ordered him to carry on with a series of verbal 'prods' (such as 'the experiment requires you continue'). The shocks went up in 15-volt increments to 450 volts, which was given 3 times per teacher. Initially happy to take part, the learner then began to protest and at 300 volts refused to answer more questions. At 315 volts he screamed loudly and was not heard from again. 100 per cent of participants obeyed up to 300 volts and 62.5 per cent went to 450 volts, even though some wept, some argued, and 3 had seizures. It was concluded that obeying authority figures is usual in a hierarchically arranged society, even when orders violate moral codes.

Description

Obedience is defined as *'complying with the demands of an authority figure'*. Milgram, from a New York Jewish family that fled Europe before the Holocaust, and a student of Asch's, was interested in understanding how 10 million Jews and Gypsies were exterminated on the orders of the Nazis during the Holocaust. He set out to test the 'Germans are different' hypothesis, which argued that the Holocaust occurred because Germans

OTHER STUDIES

- Sheridan & King (1972), by using a puppy receiving real electric shocks, tested the idea that Milgram's participants obeyed because they knew the procedure was false. 53 per cent of male participants and 100 per cent of female participants obeyed to the maximum voltage, suggesting that Milgram's results were valid and that females are more obedient.

- Burger (2009) developed an ethically acceptable variation of Milgram's study, with participants explicitly given the right to withdraw. Using males and females, an obedience rate of 70 per cent was found, suggesting that Milgram's study can be conducted ethically and that obedience rates have not changed in the 50 years since Milgram's study.

- Hofling et al. (1966) tested obedience in the real world, getting a pretend doctor to order real nurses to give an apparent overdose to a patient. 21 out of 22 obeyed, suggesting that obedience to destructive orders from a legitimate authority does occur in the real world.

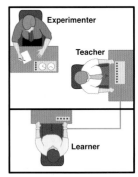

'I observed a mature and initially poised businessman enter the laboratory smiling and confident. Within 20 minutes he was reduced to a twitching, stuttering wreck, who was rapid approaching nervous collapse. He constantly pulled on his ear lobe, and twisted his hands. At one point he pushed his fist into his forehea and muttered "Oh God, let's stop it". And yet h continued to respond to every word of the experimenter, and obeyed to the end.'

Fig 1.5 The Milgram experiment set up

- ✔ Milgram's is a *paradigm study* (the accepted method of researching obedience), which has allowed comparison of obedience rates in different countries, between genders, ages and occupations.
- ✔ Valuable knowledge about obedience was gained; 74 per cent of Milgram's participants said they learned something useful about themselves. Only 2 per cent regretted being involved.
- ✔ Over 50 years later, Milgram's study continues to fascinate new generations of psychology students, illustrating its long-lasting impact.

blindly obey authority figures. Milgram showed that people are more obedient than they realise, getting participants to apparently carry out painful acts against an unobjectionable stranger purely because a researcher ordered them to. Many objected to the researcher's commands, but obeyed them to the end, showing that individuals do not necessarily agree with orders that they obediently carry out.

✘ Negative evaluation

- ✘ Milgram's study is unethical. It involves: (1) deceit through confederates believing the shocks were real and that the study involved learning and memory; (2) a lack of informed consent, as deceit was used; (3) no right of withdrawal; (4) psychological harm. Milgram argued that participants could withdraw, as 37.5 per cent of them did; also that the harm was only short-term, was reduced by debriefing and made justifiable by the valuable findings.
- ✘ Orne & Holland (1968) believed that Milgram's study lacked *internal validity*, as participants knew the shocks were fake. However, 80 per cent of participants had 'no doubts' about the authenticity of the study.
- ✘ Rank & Jacobsen (1977) argued that Hofling *et al.*'s study lacks external validity. Their more realistic replication, which allowed nurses to consult each other and used Valium, a familiar drug, saw only an 11 per cent obedience rate.

Practical application

The knowledge gained from Milgram's study is used to teach people to recognise and resist attempts to get them to obey destructive orders. Trainee aeroplane pilots undergo simulations where captains give wrongful orders so that they learn how to resist such potentially destructive commands.

pp. 17–25

1 Social influence
Explanations for obedience

Focal study

Milgram (1974) reported on several variations of his study that were designed to identify important variables associated with obedience. In a *remote authority* variation, where the confederate researcher was not in the same room as the real participant, but gave his orders over a telephone, obedience declined from the 62.5 per cent seen in the original study to 20.5 per cent. This suggests that participants were in the *autonomous state* (the opposite end of the *agentic state*) and saw themselves as responsible for their actions. In his original 1963 study, Milgram argued that many participants showed moral strain, for example 3 had seizures, but continued to obey, which suggests they were in an agentic state and felt they had to keep obeying the higher-ranked authority figure. Some participants showed no harm themselves, ignored the learner's distress and concentrated on 'doing their duty', thus seemingly recognising the legitimate authority of the researcher.

Description

Situational explanations focus on environmental factors associated with obedience.

The *agentic state* (part of the *agency* theory) is one such explanation, which sees humans as socialised from an early age to learn that obedience is necessary to maintain social order. This involves individuals seeing themselves as agents of an authority figure and thus giving up and transferring personal responsibility onto that authority figure. (The opposite state in the agency theory is the *autonomous state*, where individuals see themselves as personally responsible for their actions.) The agentic state occurs in hierarchical social systems (where people are in ranks),

OTHER STUDIES

- Tarnow (2000) found that a major contributory factor to 80 per cent of aeroplane accidents was co-pilots feeling that they could not challenge wrong decisions by the captain, due to the perceived power and legitimacy of his authority. This suggests that the perception of legitimate authority helps explain obedient behaviour.

- Hamilton (1978), in a replication of Milgram's study, found that when participants were told they were responsible for what happened, their obedience reduced. This suggests that an increase in personal responsibility and the autonomous state leads to a reduction in obedience.

- The Centre of Risk (2000) reported on how 18-year old Wayne Jowett, on remission for leukaemia, died when a doctor wrongly ordered a toxic drug to be injected into his spine and a junior doctor obeyed, even though he knew the order to be wrong. This illustrates the strength of the legitimacy of authority.

Fig 1.6 Wayne Jowett died after a junior doctor unquestioningly obeyed the wrongful orders of a more senior colleague

✔ The socialisation process – whereby people learn to obey legitimate authority figures with higher perceived status – can have a beneficial effect, as it enables hierarchical groups to function effectively. This allows meaningful social life within and between groups to occur.

✔ Milgram's variations allowed explanations for obedience to be highlighted, thereby identifying the reasons why people obey and allowing a deeper understanding of the phenomenon.

with people obeying those of perceived higher ranks.

The *legitimacy of authority* is another situational explanation, where individuals accept the power and status of authority figures to give orders, which should be obeyed, as such figures are seen as being 'in charge'. This links to the agency theory, as individuals are again seen as being socialised to accept that obedience to authority helps maintain social order. Individuals learn from experience examples of social roles relating to 'master and servant' relationships, such as parent–child, worker–boss etc., which involve accepting that we have a 'duty' to obey those higher in a social hierarchy.

✖ The agentic state involves individuals giving up some of their *free will* (their conscious control over their thoughts and actions) and therefore their behaviour becomes determined by unconscious forces outside their control. Milgram commented that when his students watched a film of his study they said they would never follow such orders and yet a few months later some of them enlisted in the army to serve in the Vietnam War and follow orders to kill people.

✖ Being in the agentic state and following the orders of a legitimate authority involves being *deindividuated*, that is losing self-awareness, which can result in individuals performing actions with negative consequences that go against their moral code.

✖ As well as situational explanations, there are *dispositional* explanations, such as gender and culture, which focus on personality characteristics that influence obedience.

Practical application

Due to cases such as that of Wayne Jowett (see **page 12**), staff in institutions like hospitals are now trained to follow official procedures and to have the confidence to challenge wrongful orders from legitimate authority figures, so that similar tragic events do not occur again.

pp. 26–8

1 Social influence
Situational variables affecting obedience

Focal study

Bickman (1974) investigated the effect uniforms have on obedience. In his study, a researcher, dressed either in civilian clothes, as a milkman, or as a security guard, ordered people in the street to pick up rubbish that they had not dropped, loan a coin to a stranger, or to move away from a bus stop. Overall, he found 14 per cent of participants obeyed when the researcher dressed as a milkman, 19 per cent when he dressed in civilian clothes and 38 per cent when he dressed as a security guard. This supports the idea that people obey those in uniform, as it gives them an increased sense of legitimate authority. In a variation of the study, Bickman found that people still obeyed the researcher when dressed as a security guard, even if he walked away after giving the order. This further illustrates the power of uniforms in increasing a sense of legitimate authority.

OTHER STUDIES

- Milgram (1974) reported that in a variation of his study, when the teacher and learner were in the same room so that the teacher could see the learner's distress, obedience declined from the 62.5 per cent seen in the original study to 40 per cent. When the teacher had to force the learner's hand onto a pretend shock-plate, obedience declined further to 30 per cent. This illustrates the effect of proximity on obedience levels.

- Milgram (1974) reported that another variation, performed in a run-down office, saw obedience fall from 62.5 per cent down to 47.5 per cent when performed in high-status Yale University. This illustrates how location can affect the degree of legitimacy that an authority figure has to deliver orders.

- In Milgram's (1963) study the confederate researcher wore a laboratory coat, which gave him a sense of increased legitimacy of authority and is assumed to have contributed to the high overall obedience rate.

Description

Situational variables form an *external* explanation of obedience, where aspects of the environment are seen as affecting obedience. Milgram's variations (see Other studies) identified several important situational variables. One such variable is *proximity*, which concerns how aware individuals are of the consequences of obedient behaviour. The closer the proximity individuals have to the consequences of obedient behaviour that has a negative outcome, the less able they are to separate themselves from such consequences and the more likely it is that obedience rates will be lower. For example, most people find it easier to obey an order to press a button that releases a missile that kills people hundreds of miles

Fig 1.7 Uniforms give a sense of legitimacy to authority

✓ Bickman's 1974 study occurred in a real-life setting and so is high in *ecological validity*. Participants did not even know they were in a study, which implies their actions were not artificial.

✓ Milgram's variations turn each study into an experiment (something the original study is not) as they create independent variables (IVs) through comparison with the findings from his standard procedure. For example, when the learner is in the same room as the teacher, it creates an IV of whether the learner was visually present or not.

✓ Milgram's variations isolate individual situational variables, allowing us to see their specific effects on obedience levels.

away, than obey an order to shoot someone, as the proximity from the consequences of such behaviour would be much closer when shooting someone up close. Another such variable is *location*, with people likely to be more obedient in environments/situations that add to the level of perceived legitimacy that an authority figure issuing orders has. For example, obedience will be higher in institutional rather than non-institutional settings, as with a teacher in a school. An additional variable is *uniforms*, as the wearing of uniforms gives an impression of increased legitimacy to an authority figure issuing orders, as with an army officer.

✗ Orne & Holland (1968) argued that Milgram's studies lacked *internal validity*, because participants knew the shocks were fake. However, 80 per cent said they had 'no doubts' about the authenticity of the study

✗ Other situational variables exist too, like *entrapment*, where participants were increasingly 'sucked into' the study by being told to give shocks of ever-increasing voltages. As the voltage of the shocks they gave increased, not obeying became increasingly difficult.

✗ Participants may also have obeyed due to *dehumanisation* (degrading people by lessening their human qualities). Milgram (1963) reported that some participants made comments like 'that guy in there was so stupid he deserved to be shocked'.

Practical application
The knowledge gained from studying situational variables has helped psychologists to form methods and strategies for resisting obedience (and conformity), such as the provision of social support.

pp. 29–30

1 Social influence

The dispositional explanation of the authoritaria personality (AP)

Focal study

Adorno *et al.* (1950) designed a questionnaire to measure levels of AP. Nine personality dimensions were assessed: *conventionalism, authoritarian submission, authoritarian aggression, superstition, power and toughness, stereotyping, destructiveness and cynicism, anti-intraception,* and *sexuality*. The questionnaire was given to 2,000 Americans, with 30 questions in total, such as '*Obedience and respect for authority are the most important virtues children should learn*'. The degree to which individuals agreed with such statements was measured, so that individuals' attitudes towards religious and ethnic minorities, as well as political, economic and moral views, could be determined. A sub-sample of 1 in 10 participants, comprising the most and least prejudiced, with an equal number of males and females, was compared in order to identify factors that gave rise to an AP. These proved to be: a strong belief in absolute obedience, submitting to authority figures, and a mistrust of minorities – supporting the idea that certain personality characteristics are associated with high obedience.

Description

The *dispositional* explanation is an *internal* explanation, as it centres on the idea that certain internal personality characteristics are associated with high levels of obedience (as opposed to the situational explanation, which believes *external* situational factors determine obedience levels). The *authoritarian personality* (AP) was proposed by Fromm (1941) as an attempt to categorise individuals who held right-wing, conservative views. He saw such individuals as having a belief in unquestioning obedience, submission to authority and domination of minorities. Adorno *et al.* (1950) additionally saw such individuals as having insecurities, formed in childhood through having domineering, authoritarian (controlling)

OTHER STUDIES

- Zillmer *et al.* (1995) examined the personality characteristics of 16 Nazi war criminals (comprising both high-ranking officers and lower-ranking soldiers), who were tried at the Nuremberg trials after the Second World War, to ascertain whether a 'Nazi personality' existed – similar to Fromm's idea of the AP. The Nazis scored high on 3 of the 9 F-scale dimensions, but not on all 9 as expected, giving limited support for the concept of an AP.

- Elms & Milgram (1966) found that highly obedient participants in Milgram's study scored significantly higher for authoritarianism on the F-scale than participants who disobeyed and refused to deliver shocks. These findings give stronger support for the idea of an AP that makes people more unquestioningly obedient.

- Altemeyer (1988) found that participants who scored high on the F-scale, who were ordered to give themselves shocks, gave stronger shocks than those who scored low on the F-scale, providing additional support to the existence of an AP type.

✔ Supporting research for the AP shows that dispositional factors (personality) affect obedience levels, as well as situational factors. However, for the best understanding of obedience behaviour, dispositional and situational factors should be considered together.

✔ Milgram found situational factors were stronger than dispositional ones, which led him to conclude that the 'Germans are different' hypothesis was wrong (that Germans have personality traits that make them highly obedient to destructive orders – see **page 10**). However, research into the AP suggests that some people might be more naturally obedient than others, though whether this can be generalised to all people of a certain culture is debatable.

parents, which led them to be hostile to non-conventional people and to have a belief in the need for power and toughness that made them very obedient to authority figures. In order to measure an individual's level of AP, Adorno created the F-scale questionnaire (the 'F' stands for fascist). It has 30 questions that assess 9 personality dimensions. More recently, Jost *et al.* (2003) suggested a more cognitive explanation of AP. They saw it as being motivated by thought processes that underpin a desire to reduce the anxieties and fears that social change brings – obedience is seen to help prevent such disruptive social change.

✖ Negative evaluation

✖ Hyman & Sheatsley (1954) found that lower educational level was a better explanation of high F-scale scores than an authoritarian personality. Cultural and social norms have also been shown to be better predictors of prejudice than personality variables.

✖ Authoritarian individuals do not always score high on F-scale dimensions, while domineering parents do not always produce children with an AP. Nor can the AP explain why individuals may be prejudiced against some minorities, but not others. This lowers support for the concept.

✖ The theory is also politically biased, as it has a negative viewpoint of individuals who hold right-wing, conservative views.

Practical application

If the concept of the AP being a negative personality type formed in childhood is valid, then promoting less domineering and controlling parenting styles should result in fewer people developing the personality type. This in turn should result in the creation of more individuals able to resist orders with potentially negative consequences.

pp. 30–2

1 Social influence
Explanations of resistance to social influence

Focal study

Avtgis (1998) conducted a meta-analysis of studies involving LoC and conformity, in which the average effect size for internal and external LoC was measured. Earlier research had indicated that those scoring high on internal LoC are less easily persuadable, less socially influenced and less conformist than those who score high on external LoC. After subjecting the data to statistical analysis, it was found that these predictions were generally true, with participants who displayed an internal LoC being less easily influenced and therefore more able to resist conformity. These results support the idea that differences in conformist behaviour are related to differences in measures of LoC, which suggests that differences in LoC are linked to differences in the ability to resist social influence.

OTHER STUDIES

- Asch (1956) (see **page 2**) found that if a confederate dissenter answered correctly from the start of his study, conformity dropped from the usual 32 per cent to 5.5 per cent, but if the confederate only dissented later in the study conformity only dropped to 8.5 per cent. This suggests social support received earlier is more effective than that received later.

- Milgram (1974) in a variation of his study found that when 2 confederate teachers refused to obey and left the study, only 10 per cent of participants gave the maximum shocks, which suggests that *disobedient models* are a powerful source of social support, as they reduce the unanimity of a situation. This makes it easier for an individual to act independently.

- Shute (1975) found that students with an internal LoC, exposed to peers expressing pro-drug attitudes, conformed less to such pro-drug attitudes than students with an external LoC. This supports the idea that having an internal LoC increases resistance to social influence.

Description

The consequences of conforming and obeying, although often positive for society, can sometimes be negative. Therefore, it is important that psychologists, as well as understanding why people conform and obey, also know how such social influences can be resisted. Effective strategies for resistance can then be formulated.

One important explanation of resistance is that of *social support*, which involves the perception of assistance and solidarity being available from others. If dissenters (people who go against the attitudes and behaviour of the group) are present in a social group, they break up the *unanimity* of the group, making it easier for individuals to resist social influence to conform and obey. This works even if a dissenter displays a different

Fig 1.8 Whistle-blowers who report illegal activities within institutions tend to have a high internal LoC

✔ Many studies into social support – such as Asch's variations that concentrated specifically on the role of dissent – are experiments, which isolate and rigorously test individual variables. This demonstrates such variables' specific effects – in Asch's studies, on the ability to resist social influences of conformity and obedience.

✔ The extensive knowledge gained from research into conformity and obedience can be used to formulate and teach effective strategies to help individuals to resist social pressures to conform and obey in situations with potentially negative consequences. Even just being taught about studies like Asch's and Milgram's can help people recognise and therefore resist similar attempts to manipulate their social behaviour.

attitude or behaviour to one preferred by a given individual who also privately disagrees with the group.

Another important explanation is that of *locus of control* (LoC), which involves the extent to which things happen as a result of an individual's choices and decisions. Internal LoC involves the belief that things happen due to internally controlled factors, such as effort, while external LoC involves the belief that things happen as a result of fate and other uncontrollable external forces. Rotter (1966) argued that a high internal LoC made individuals more resistant to social influence, as such individuals see themselves as having a free choice over whether to conform or obey.

✘ Most research into LoC involves correlations, which do not show causality. Therefore, the direction of the relationship is not known (for example, resisting social influence may create a higher internal LoC, rather than a high internal LoC, making people able to resist social influence). Other non-measured variables may be involved too.

✘ Asch (1956) found that even if a dissenter gave a different wrong answer to other confederates, conformity dropped from 32 per cent to 9 per cent, which suggests it is the reduction in the majority's agreement, rather than the social support given by the dissenter, which is the important factor in resisting social influence.

Practical application

Chui (2004) reports that 'whistle-blowers' (people within institutions who report illegal activities) have a high internal LoC. Therefore, it would be useful for institutions to appoint such people to investigate possible instances of corporate fraud, like paying bribes, money laundering and covering up institutional abuses, such as avoidable hospital deaths.

pp. 33–40

1 Social influence
Minority influence

OTHER STUDIES

- Nemeth (1986) had groups of three participants and one confederate, who were asked to consider how much compensation to pay to an accident victim. When confederates consistently argued for a low amount, they had no effect on the majority, but when they compromised and offered a slightly higher amount, the majority changed their opinion and lowered their original amount. This suggests flexibility is more important than consistency in minority influence.

- Mugny & Papastamou (1982) found that minorities who refused to budge on opinions about controlling pollution, were not persuasive, but flexible minorities were. This supports the idea that flexibility is more influential than consistency.

- Smith et al. (1996) found that if a minority could get a majority to consider an issue in terms of the arguments for and against the issue, then the minority became more influential. This suggests that *systematic processing* (thinking deeply about something) is also an important factor in minority influence.

Description

Minority influence is a type of social influence that motivates individuals to reject established majority group norms. This is achieved through *conversion*, where individuals become gradually won over to a minority viewpoint. Conversion requires a permanent change in an individual's belief system and a new belief/behaviour being accepted both privately and publicly. This involves *internalisation* (see **page 3**) and as such is a strong, true form of conformity. Conversion generally occurs through *informational social influence*, where a minority exposes the majority to new information and ideas. This is a gradual process, where individuals

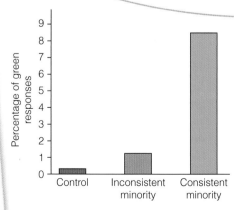

Fig 1.9 Bar chart showing conformity to inconsistent and consistent minority influence

✓ Moscovici *et al.*'s findings that consistent minorities have greater social influence on majorities than inconsistent minorities have been shown to be valid, as they have support from other studies. For example, Meyers *et al.* (2000) found that minority groups successful in affecting minorities were more consistent than inconsistent minority groups.

✓ Minority influence has an important role to play in social influence. Without minority influence, important social change, innovation and the introduction of new ideas and practices cannot occur (see **page 22**).

rethink their belief systems in regard to such new information and ideas. It is known as *social cryptoamnesia*, where initial converts are few, but then there are more and more converts as the minority gets bigger, acquiring more status, power and acceptability. Minority influence is most persuasive if the minority has a behavioural style that is: (1) *consistent*, as this suggests the minority has confidence in its beliefs; (2) *committed*, as this shows the minority may have resisted social pressures, ridicule and abuse against their beliefs; (3) *flexible*, as this suggests the minority can be moderate, co-operative and reasonable enough to show some compromise.

❌ **Negative evaluation**

✗ Moscovici *et al.*'s study lacks external validity, as asking participants to identify the colour of slides is artificial and not true to life. Moscovici *et al.* also only used females as participants in their study, so findings cannot be generalised to males.

✗ Studies into minority influence that use confederates pretending to be minorities are unethical. They involve deceit, which means it is not possible for participants to give informed consent. Participants may also experience mild stress in such studies.

✗ Studies into minority influence also often fail to identify important variables like group size, status and the minority group's degree of organisation.

Practical application

Because minority influence needs careful consideration and changes in beliefs and behaviour occur over time, new, innovative practices can be road-tested for suitability. This means that any unforeseen dangers of a new practice should emerge before it becomes a mainstream practice, for example, the adoption of euthanasia (voluntary ending of life) as an accepted practice.

pp. 41–4

1 Social influence
The role of social influence processes in social change

Focal study

Martin *et al.* (2007) investigated whether opinions given by minority or majority group influence are more resistant to conflicting opinions. Forty-eight participants, who were initially supportive of voluntary euthanasia, received 2 messages. The first was the *pro-attitudinal message*, which gave 6 arguments **against** voluntary euthanasia and was supported by either minority or majority group influence. The second was the *counter-attitudinal message*, which gave 6 arguments **for** voluntary euthanasia. Attitudes were then measured. When the pro-attitudinal message was supported by minority influence, attitudes were more resistant to change. This suggests that minority influence creates *systematic processing* (consideration) of its viewpoints, leading to attitudes resistant to counter-persuasion. Therefore, the opinions of minorities are subjected to higher-level processing than those of majorities. The findings also suggest that minority influence leads to social change through systematic processing, causing changes to belief systems that lead to changes in viewpoints and behaviour.

Description

Social change is the process by which society changes beliefs, attitudes and behaviour to create new social norms (expected ways of behaviour and thinking).

Minority influence is the main force for social change, with minority viewpoints slowly winning the majority over to accept new social norms. Minority influence acts slowly, involving *systematic processing* (thought processes) that changes belief systems. It is therefore resistant to change.

Majority influence is more immediate and unthinking. Its main role is to help maintain social order by getting people to conform to social norms which have already been established through minority influence.

OTHER STUDIES

- Martin & Hewstone (1999) found that minority influence leads to more creative and novel outcomes than majority influence, which supports the idea that minority, rather than majority, influence is a greater force for innovation and change.

- Burgoon (1995) reported that it is the unexpected and unusual behaviours exhibited by minority groups that are alerting and attention-grabbing, and which lead to deep-level analysis of such behaviours and ideas. This suggests that it is the breaking of social norms by minorities that leads to systematic processing and ultimately to social change.

- Nemeth (2009) reported that it is the 'dissent' of minorities to accepted social norms that 'opens' individual's minds to search for information and consider other choices, which ultimately makes them more creative, better informed and better able to make decisions. This demonstrates how the resistance of minorities to conform to and obey social norms acts as a starting point for social change to occur.

Fig 1.10 Would an argument against voluntary euthanasia be more resistant to change if supported by a minority or a majority group?

✔ Rather than viewing majority influence, minority influence and obedience as working independently of each other, a more constructive view – allowing greater understanding of the role of social influence processes in social change – is to view these processes as working in combination with each other. So minority influence brings about social change in an ordered and considered manner, and majority influence and obedience oversee and regulate the new social order that minority influence creates.

✔ Research into social change mainly involves experiments, which show cause and effect relationships and allow individual variables to be isolated and tested to assess their relative roles in social change.

During the process of social change comes a moment of critical mass, whereby the minority viewpoint becomes that of the mainstream and the majority begin to conform to the new viewpoint through *compliance* (see **page 2**). This involves only public (not private) agreement, with individuals still holding their original beliefs. More permanent social change requires conformity through *identification*, where belief systems are changed.

Obedience serves like majority influence to help oversee and maintain existing social orders. Individuals who show high levels of resistance to social influence are more likely to become agents for social change by modelling the attitudes and behaviour necessary for such change to occur.

✖ Clark & Maas (1990) found no minority influence effect upon a majority group larger than 4 people, which suggests that minority influence is restricted in its ability to convert and incur social change.

✖ Many experiments into the role of social influence processes in social change lack external validity, as they often involve artificial tasks that lack relevance to real-life situations. This lowers the validity of conclusions drawn from the findings.

✖ Experiments into the role of social influence processes in social change often result in ethical issues, especially deceit, meaning that informed consent cannot be gained.

Practical application

A practical application of research into social change is that in business and industry companies should not place only 'yes men' (people who conform and obey readily) into management, as they stifle innovation. Minorities of dissenters should also be included, as they will promote an atmosphere of innovative change.

pp. 45–8

2 Memory
The multi-store model (MSM)

Focal study

Baddeley (1966) examined encoding in STM and LTM by giving 75 participants either: *acoustically similar* words (rhyming words) like 'caught' and 'taut', *acoustically dissimilar* words (non-rhyming words) like 'foul' and 'deep', *semantically similar* words (words with similar meanings) like 'big' and 'huge', or *semantically dissimilar* words (words with non-similar meanings) like 'pen' and 'ring'. With STM, acoustically dissimilar words were better recalled (80 per cent) than acoustically similar words (10 per cent), indicating acoustic encoding to be dominant. Semantically dissimilar words (71 per cent) were recalled slightly better than semantically similar ones (64 per cent), suggesting semantic coding does occur in STM but isn't dominant. With LTM, participants followed the same procedure, but with a 20-minute gap between presentation and recall. There was no difference between acoustically similar and dissimilar words, but more semantically dissimilar words (85 per cent) were recalled than semantically similar ones (55 per cent), suggesting semantic encoding is dominant in LTM.

OTHER STUDIES

- Crowder (1993) found that memories in the SR only retain information in the iconic store for a few milliseconds, but retain information for up to 3 seconds within the echoic store. This supports the idea that sensory information is coded into different stores, while additionally suggesting that sensory memories have different durations.

- Peterson & Peterson (1959) read participants nonsense trigrams (words of 3 random letters, e.g. XPJ), then asked them to count backwards from a large digit between 3 and 18 seconds later to prevent recall. 90 per cent of trigrams were recalled after 3 seconds, but only 5 per cent after 18 seconds, suggesting STM duration is between 18 and 20 seconds.

- Bahrick *et al.* (1975) found that participants who had left school in the last 15 years recalled 90 per cent of faces and names of schoolmates from photos, while those who had left 48 years previously recalled 80 per cent of names and 70 per cent of faces. This implies LTM duration to be very long-lasting.

Description

The multi-store model (MSM) explains how data (pieces of information) move between 3 storage systems, each system differing in terms of:
- *capacity* – how much information is stored
- *duration* – how long information is stored
- *encoding* – the form in which information is stored.

The *sensory register* (SR) holds huge amounts of unprocessed sensory information received by sensory organs for a short duration. Information that is paid attention to goes for further processing in *short-term memory* (STM) and non-attended information is immediately lost. The SR has separate stores for sensory inputs, e.g. *iconic*

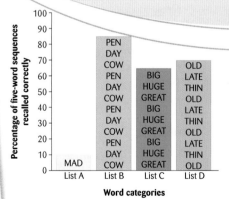

Fig 2.1 Baddeley's (1966) acoustic/semantic study findings, where List A = acoustically similar words, List B = acoustically dissimilar words, List C = semantically similar words and List D = semantically dissimilar words

- ✔ The MSM was the first cognitive explanation of memory and inspired interest and research, leading to later theories like the working memory model that gave an even greater understanding of memory.
- ✔ The brief duration of SR and STM has an evolutionary value, as we only need to focus on sensory information with an immediate survival value. LTMs are retained for longer as they may have an ongoing survival value.
- ✔ The theory is supported by amnesia cases (loss of memory). Patients lose either their STM or their LTM ability, but not both, supporting the idea that STM and LTM are separate memory stores located in different brain areas.

store for visual and *echoic store* for auditory information.

STM is a temporary memory system holding information in use. The dominant encoding type here is *acoustic*, with other sensory codes also used. Capacity is limited to 5–9 items, extended by *chunking*, where the size of the units of information is increased. Duration is limited to around 20 seconds, though rehearsal retains data within the STM loop, until eventually it becomes more permanent within *long-term memory* (LTM). The dominant encoding type in LTM is *semantic*, though other encoding types also occur, e.g. *visual* and *acoustic*. Potential capacity is assumed to be unlimited, with duration potentially lifelong. Information in LTM does not have to be continually rehearsed to be retained.

❌ Negative evaluation

- ✗ The MSM is oversimplified as seeing STM and LTM as single stores. Research suggests there are several types of STM, such as separate stores for visual and auditory information, as well as different types of LTM, such as *procedural*, *episodic* and *semantic* LTM (see **page 28**).
- ✗ Cohen (1990) thinks memory capacity is not measurable only by the amount of information, but by the nature of the information to be recalled. Some things are easier to recall regardless of the amount of information being recalled. MSM does not consider this.
- ✗ MSM focuses too much on memory structure rather than on processes.

Practical application

Research into the MSM has allowed psychologists to create strategies for improving memory performance, such as chunking, where STM capacity is increased by grouping separate pieces of information into larger units with a collective meaning. This can be useful for students when revising.

pp. 52–62

25

2 Memory
The working memory model (WMM)

Focal study

Alkhalifa (2009) examined the existence of the EB, by presenting 48 students with numerical information on a screen, either in sequential fashion (e.g. 1, 2, 3, 4) or in parallel fashion (where information was presented in different parts of the screen simultaneously). The numbers used were of sufficient complexity to override the capacities of both the PL and the VSS. Participants were set problem-solving questions based on the numbers presented. Those using sequentially presented material were superior. This suggests a limitation exists on information passing from perception to learning, as parallel processing was a hindrance to learning. As sequential processing was superior, it indicates that the capacity of the working memory (WM) is larger than that determined by the capacity of the PL and the VSS, implying the existence of a limited-capacity EB, which acts as a temporary 'general store' of integrated material.

OTHER STUDIES

- Trojani & Grossi (1995) reported the case study of 'SC', who had brain damage affecting the functioning of his PL, but not his VSS. This suggests the PL and VSS are separate systems associated with different brain areas.
- Gathercole & Baddeley (1993) found that participants had difficulty simultaneously tracking a moving point of light and describing the angles on a hollow letter 'F', as both tasks involved using the VSS. However, they had little difficulty tracking the light and performing a simultaneous verbal task, as those tasks used the VSS and the PL, indicating the VSS and PL to be separate systems.
- Alkhalifa (2009) reported a case study of a patient with severely impaired LTM, who had a STM capacity of 25 prose items, far exceeding the capacity of both the VSS and the PL. This supports the idea of an EB, which holds items in working memory until they are recalled.

Description

Replacing the single STM of the MSM (see **page 24**), the working memory model (WMM) proposes a 4-component working memory based on the form of processing each carries out.

The limited-capacity *central executive* (CE) acts as a filter, dealing with all sensory information and determining which information is attended to, and then allocating this to 'slave systems', temporary stores dealing with different types of sensory information.

The *phonological loop* (PL) is a slave system dealing with auditory information. It is similar to the rehearsal system of the MSM, with a limited capacity determined by the amount of information spoken in about 2 seconds.

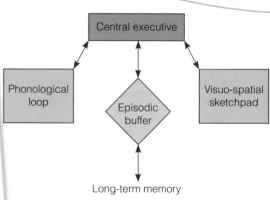

Fig 2.2 The working memory model

✔ PET scans show different brain areas are activated when individuals perform verbal and visual tasks. This supports the idea of the PL and the VSS being separate systems based within the biology of the brain.

✔ The PL is associated with the evolution of human vocal language, as the development of the PL produced an increase in the short-term ability to remember vocalisations. This helped the learning of more complex language abilities, like grammar (the rules of language) and semantics (the meanings of things).

✔ The WMM is a superior explanation of STM to the MSM, as it explains STM as having several storage systems and so is better able to explain how STM actually operates.

It divides into the *primary acoustic store* (PAS), which stores words in the order they were heard, and the *articulatory process* (AP), which permits sub-vocal repetition of information stored in the PL.

Another slave system is the *visuo-spatial sketchpad* (VSS), a temporary store for visual and spatial items and the relationships between them. It divides into the *visual cache* (VC), which stores visual material concerning form and colour, and the *inner scribe* (IS), which stores information about spatial relationships (where objects are in relationships to each other).

A slave system added to the model later on is the *episodic buffer* (EB), which is a temporary store of integrated information from the CE, PL, VSS and LTM.

❌ Negative evaluation

✘ Studies of the PL and VSS often use a *dual task technique* (doing 2 tasks at once), but the tasks performed are often ones that do not relate to everyday life (like tracking a moving dot of light) and so are artificial and thus lacking in external validity.

✘ Although the CE is seen as the most important component of the WMM (as it oversees the operation of working memory), little is known about how it works – for example, how it decides what we pay attention to.

Practical application

Children with **attention deficit hyperactivity disorder** (ADHD) often have impairments in working memory. Alloway (2006) recommends: using brief, simple instructions (so they are not forgotten); giving instructions as individual, frequently repeated steps; and getting children to periodically repeat instructions so that they stay focused.

pp. 63–8

2 Memory
Types of long-term memory (LTM)

Focal study

Tulving (1989) investigated differences in the processing of episodic and semantic memory. Six participants performed 8 successive trials involving 4 SMs and 4 EMs. During a trial, participants attempted to retrieve a self-selected memory. EMs involved personally experienced events, like a holiday, while SMs involved knowledge acquired through learning, such as from reading a book. Radioactive gold was injected into the participant 60 seconds after retrieval began and their brain was scanned 8 seconds later (after the gold had arrived in the brain). In 3 participants there was greater activation in the frontal lobes of the brain during EM retrieval and in the posterior region of the cortex during SM retrieval (3 participants produced inconclusive data). This suggests SMs and EMs involve different brain areas and are therefore separate forms of LTM.

Description

Research indicates several types of long-term memory (LTM), each with a separate function and associated with different brain areas. LTM sub-divides into *explicit* (easy to express in words), which requires conscious thought to be recalled, and *implicit* (difficult to express in words), which does not require conscious thought to be recalled.

One type of explicit LTM is *episodic memory* (EM), which gives an autobiographical record of personal experiences, like when your birthday is. Strength of EM relates to strength of emotions and the degree of processing at coding. EM helps us distinguish between real events and imagination.

A second type of explicit LTM is *semantic memory* (SM), which contains knowledge

OTHER STUDIES

- Herlitz *et al.* (1997) assessed explicit LTM abilities in 1,000 Swedish participants and found that females consistently performed better than males on tasks requiring episodic LTM, although there were no differences in SM ability. This suggests there are gender differences in EM ability, possibly because females tend to have better verbal ability.

- Finke *et al.* (2012) reported the case study of 'PM', a professional cellist who suffered severe amnesia due to damage in several brain areas through illness. His episodic and semantic LTM was so badly affected that he could not remember musical facts, but his ability to read and play music, including new pieces, was unaffected. This suggests different types of LTM are located in different brain areas.

- Van Gorp *et al.* (1999) found that abstinence from cocaine by heavy users led to a rapid increase in procedural memory ability. As abstinence from cocaine stimulates dopamine production, it suggests dopamine levels are linked to procedural LTM.

2 Memory

28

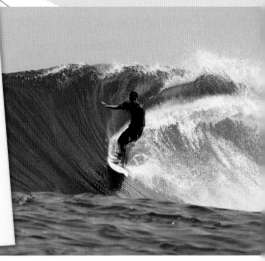

Fig 2.3 Recalling how to surf is an example of procedural LTM

✔ Episodic LTMs may differ from semantic LTMs in terms of different types of thinking and emotion, as EMs are associated with conscious awareness of events and emotional feelings related to them, while SMs are more associated with non-emotional, objective analysis of phenomena.

✔ The frontal lobe brain area's association with episodic LTMs is supported by case studies of amnesiacs with impaired episodic memories having damaged frontal lobes.

✔ Procedural memories may take longer to learn than explicit LTMs, as they often involve motor functions and spatial abilities, while explicit memories tend to involve higher-level thought processes.

learned. Strength of SM also relates to the degree of processing at coding, with SMs generally longer lasting than EMs. SMs link to EMs, as new knowledge (SMs) is generally learned from specific experiences (EMs). Over time, such memories become less episodic and more semantic.

Procedural memory (PM) is a type of implicit LTM, allowing us to perform learned tasks with little conscious thought, for example surfing. Many PMs concern motor skills, like walking, and are learned early in life. PMs are also involved in language, helping individuals to speak and use grammar without thinking how to. As PMs do not need conscious thought, we can simultaneously perform other cognitive tasks requiring attention.

✖ Negative evaluation

✖ The extent to which episodic and semantic LTM systems are different is unclear. Although different brain areas are involved, there is also a lot of overlap between the 2 systems, with semantic LTMs often emerging from episodic LTMs. Therefore, it is not known whether or not the gradual transformation of an EM into a SM involves a change in memory systems.

✖ As only 3 out of Tulving's 6 participants showed differences in the processing of semantic and episodic LTMs, the findings cannot be generalised. Also, as 2 of the participants were Tulving and his wife, the findings may be prone to researcher bias.

Practical application

Psychologists at Vanderbilt University have programmed EM into a robot, so that it can recall past experiences to help solve problems. Attempts are now being made to give it an episodic buffer (see **page 27**) so it can combine information from different sensory memory channels like a human does.

pp. 69–75

2 Memory

Explanations for forgetting

Focal study

Schmidt et al. (2000) investigated the influence of retroactive interference on the memory of street names learned in childhood. 211 Dutch participants aged 11 to 79 years were given a map of Molenberg, where they had gone to school, with 48 street names replaced with numbers. Participants had to recall as many names as possible. Other relevant details were also collected, such as how many times they had moved house, where they had lived and for how long, how often they visited Molenberg etc. The amount of retroactive interference was assessed by how many times participants had moved to other neighbourhoods (and therefore learned new sets of street names). A positive correlation was found between the number of times participants had moved neighbourhoods outside of Molenberg and the number of street names forgotten. This suggests retroactive interference, as learning new sets of street names makes recalling old sets difficult.

OTHER STUDIES

- Peterson & Peterson (1959) gave participants meaningless words of 3 letters and got them to count backwards aloud to prevent rehearsal. After 18 seconds only 5 per cent of participants showed correct recall. This illustrates how memories fade over time, and suggests that forgetting may be due to information no longer being in storage, as well as to retrieval problems.

- Darley et al. (1973) found that participants who had hidden money while they were high on marijuana could not recall where they had put it, but they could when they were high again. This supports the idea that forgetting occurs when internal context of retrieval differs from that of coding, as stated by state-dependent learning.

- Abernethy (1940) found that students recalled information best when in the room they had learned the material in with their usual teacher, rather than in an unfamiliar room with an unfamiliar teacher. This supports the idea of forgetting occurring when external context of retrieval differs from that of coding, as stated by context-dependent failure.

Description

Forgetting is the failure to retrieve memories, with information either no longer in, or unable to be retrieved from, storage. *Interference theory* sees material becoming confused with, or disrupted by, other information during coding, leading to inaccurate recall. *Proactive interference*, which works forwards in time, occurs where information previously stored interferes with attempts to recall new information. For example, the memory of your old phone number disrupts attempts to recall your new phone number. *Retroactive interference*, which works backwards in time, occurs when coding of new information disrupts previously stored information. For example, the memory of your new password prevents recall

Fig 2.4 Street map of Molenberg in Holland

- ✔ Schmidt et al.'s (2000) street name study is especially useful, as it involves a real-life scenario and therefore has high external validity.
- ✔ Schmidt et al.'s methodology can also quite easily be adapted to assess the effect of proactive, as well as retroactive, interference.
- ✔ Cue-dependent theory is regarded as the best explanation of forgetting in LTM, due to the huge amount of supportive research the explanation has, which shows the importance of retrieval cues in facilitating accurate recall.

of your old password. *Cue-dependent forgetting* sees recall as dependent upon *retrieval cues* (prompts that facilitate recall). Forgetting occurs if the retrieval cue under which a memory is stored cannot be accessed. *Context-dependent failure* occurs with *external* retrieval cues, where forgetting occurs as the external environment is different at recall from how it was at coding. For example, you may perform worse in an exam sat in an unfamiliar room than in the room where you learned the material. *State-dependent failure* occurs with *internal* retrieval cues, where forgetting occurs because an individual's internal environment is dissimilar to that when the information was coded. For example, a person may fail when sober to recall information that was learned when drunk.

❌ **Negative evaluation**

- ✗ There are a number of extraneous variables in Schmidt et al.'s (2000) study. For example, participants who played a lot in the streets of Molenberg as children, or who walked to school, may have learned street names to a greater extent and therefore would have had better recall than those who did not play in the streets or went to school by car.

- ✗ Interference theory only explains forgetting when 2 sets of information are similar, like simultaneously learning 2 languages at school. This does not happen that often and so cannot explain the majority of forgetting.

- ✗ Although studies show interference to be a real effect, they do not identify the cognitive processes at work, which means the explanation is incomplete.

Practical application

One practical application of the interference explanation of forgetting is that, wherever possible, in order to cut down on retrieval failures, students should sit an exam in the room where they learned the material, so that the context of retrieval is the same as that of coding.

pp. 76–84

2 Memory

Factors affecting the accuracy of eyewitness testimony (EWT)

Focal study

Loftus & Pickrell (2003) investigated whether false memories could be created through the use of post-event information. 120 participants who had visited Disneyland as children were placed into 4 groups. They were asked to evaluate some advertising copy about Disneyland and answer questions about their visit there. Group 1 read fake copy featuring no cartoon characters; Group 2 read the fake copy featuring no cartoon characters but there was a large figure of Bugs Bunny (a Warner Brothers character) in their room; Group 3 read the fake copy which now featured Bugs Bunny; Group 4 read the fake copy featuring Bugs Bunny and also had the large figure in the room. 30 per cent of participants in Group 3 and 40 per cent of participants in Group 4 recalled meeting Bugs Bunny at Disneyland – some even recalled having their photo taken with him. This suggests that post-event information can be misleading so that false memories are created.

OTHER STUDIES

- Ginet & Verkampt (2007) found that participants made moderately anxious by being told that fake electrodes on their bodies produced electric shocks in response to incorrect answers had better recall of a traffic accident viewed on video than participants with low anxiety through being told the electrodes simply monitored bodily activity. This supports the inverted-U hypothesis.

- Loftus & Palmer (1974) found that participants' estimates of car speeds viewed on a video were affected by which verb they were given in a question asking 'How fast were the cars going when they *contacted/hit/bumped/collided/smashed* each other?' This illustrates how misleading information in the form of leading questions can affect EWT.

- Koehler *et al.* (2002) found that participants were less able to recall stressful words than non-stressful words, supporting the concept of repression. However, Hadley & MacKay (2006) found that stressful words were better recalled, as they are more memorable, which suggests the case for repression is not proven.

Description

Eyewitness testimony (EWT) concerns the accuracy of recall of those present at an event when it occurred. It is especially important in courts of law.

Bartlett (1932) detailed how *schemas*, ways of perceiving the world formed from experience, affect EWT, as memories are not accurate 'snapshots' but reconstructions of what we believe happened in an event based on previous experience, stereotypes, mood etc.

Misleading information can affect EWT, first through *leading questions*, which suggest a certain answer to a witness, and also through *post-event discussion*, where misleading information is

Fig 2.5 This image of Bugs Bunny was used in the study by Loftus & Pickrell to produce a fake memory

✔ Loftus & Pickrell's (2003) Bugs Bunny study can be regarded as superior to the more famous Loftus & Palmer (1974) study, as it uses memory of a real-life event, visiting Disneyland as a child, and therefore has higher external validity.

✔ Research into EWT has led to changes in court procedures. The Devlin report (1976) led to convictions based on uncorroborated EWT (where there is only one independent EWT) being disallowed.

✔ Loftus has performed many studies over many years which have produced a wealth of information that has increased our understanding of how false memories can be created.

added to a memory after an event has been witnessed.

The witnessing of real-life events can often involve *anxiety*, which can severely affect the quality of recall. The *Yerkes–Dodson inverted-U hypothesis* explains how low and high levels of anxiety are both associated with poor recall in terms of detail and accuracy of events witnessed, while moderate anxiety is associated with good recall.

Anxiety can also affect the quality of recall through *repression*, where traumatic events become hidden in the unconscious mind so that a witness is unaware of them and cannot recall them. Repression, however, is a controversial idea and few psychologists see it as a valid concept.

❌ **Negative evaluation**

✗ Many studies of the effects of anxiety on EWT are laboratory based and therefore not generalisable. Real-life studies often find different results, e.g. Yuille & Cutshall (1986) found that high anxiety produced excellent recall of a real armed robbery, thereby refuting the inverted-U hypothesis.

✗ Loftus & Palmer's findings may be due to demand characteristics, not leading questions, as participants may have given answers they thought the researchers wanted, rather than their actual recollections.

✗ Participants do not expect to be misled by researchers, so inaccurate recall in studies may be due to participants believing researchers' misleading statements to be true.

Practical application

One practical application of research into EWT is in advertising, where advertisers use post-event information (usually through fake nostalgic images) to try and create false positive memories of products, so that we will buy them.

pp. 86–91

2 Memory

Improving the accuracy of eyewitness testimony (EWT)

Focal study

Meissner & Fraser (2010) performed a meta-analysis of studies of the CI, including the ECI and the MCI, to assess their relative effectiveness. They reviewed 57 studies involving comparison of the CI with a control technique, such as the SPI, that had been published in peer reviewed journals. 32 per cent of the studies used the CI, 23 per cent the ECI and 45 per cent the MCI. The CI was found to produce more accurate detail than non-CI techniques, though there was a small increase in inaccurate details with the CI. The MCI produced more inaccurate details than the CI or the ECI and also produced slightly more false memories. This suggests that CIs are superior, as they produce more accurate, detailed information than non-CI techniques. The CI technique is therefore an effective means of conducting interviews, though some inaccurate detail is noticeable.

Description

One strategy for improving EWT is the *cognitive interview* (CI). Replacing the *standard police interview* (SPI), which depended on free recall of events, it is an interview procedure facilitating accurate, detailed recall, based on Tulving's (1974) idea that several retrieval paths to memory exist. The CI also makes use of Tulving & Thomson's *encoding specificity theory* (1973), which suggests the use of as many retrieval cues as possible to improve recall. The CI has 4 components:

1 *change of narrative order* – events being recalled in different chronological orders, e.g. from end to beginning

2 *change of perspective* – events being recalled from different perspectives, e.g. from the offender's point of view

OTHER STUDIES

- Verkampt & Ginet (2010) interviewed children after a painting session, and found that the CI and 4 types of MCI were superior to the SPI in producing accurate detail and that versions of the MCI that removed the 'change of narrative' component were most superior. This suggests that specific versions of the MCI are most appropriate for certain types of witnesses.

- Holliday (2003) gave children either a SPI or a MCI, specially designed for children, after showing them a video of a child's birthday party. She found that the MCI produced more accurate detail than the SPI, demonstrating the effectiveness of MCIs with children.

- Milne & Bull (2002) found the 'report everything' and 'context reinstatement' components of the CI to be the key techniques in gaining accurate, detailed recall, which implies that some components of the CI are more effective than others.

Fig 2.6 The modified cognitive interview is often used to allow police officers to interview children

✔ The CI has potential uses within other organisations, not just the police, where accurate memory is necessary – for example, in the army, where debriefing of soldiers after active combat incidents is used to gain valid recollections.

✔ Fisher & Geiselman (1988) have continued to develop the CI using information gained from watching 'good' and 'poor' interviewers. This has led to more open-ended questions and fitting the order of questioning to the witness's order of experience, increasing accuracy of recall from 40 per cent to 60 per cent.

✔ Variations of the CI have proven to be effective with specific groups of people in generating accurate witness recall of incidents.

3 *mental reinstatement of context* – making use of environmental context, e.g. weather and emotional context (feelings) of the crime scene

4 *report everything* – all information is recalled, even trivial or muddled content.

Fisher *et al.* (1987) produced the *enhanced cognitive interview* (ECI) to overcome problems caused by inappropriate sequencing of questions. Extra features include: (a) *minimisation of distraction,* (b) *reduction of anxiety,* (c) *getting witnesses to speak slowly,* (d) *asking open-ended questions.* The *modified cognitive interview* (MCI) is a shortened version of the CI technique, which is often preferred by police forces as it takes less operational time. MCIs usually omit the 'change narrative order' and 'change perspective' components.

✖ Negative evaluation

✖ Many police forces have problems using the CI, as it is too time-consuming for practical use. This has led to poorer or rushed versions of the technique being used, which can be less effective. The production of confabulations (false memories) is also problematic for police usage.

✖ A limitation of CIs is that they are not generally effective as a method of memory enhancement for recognition of suspects from identity parades or photographs.

✖ Police forces use widely differing versions of the SPI, making objective comparisons difficult to achieve.

Practical application

MCIs can be used with children. Omitting the 'change perspective' component is useful here, as children are often too young to see things from others' point of view. Other groups of witnesses, like those with learning difficulties, can also be interviewed effectively with specifically designed forms of the MCI.

pp. 92–8

3 Attachment
Caregiver–infant interactions in humans

Focal study

Papousek *et al.* (1991) investigated whether 'caregiverese' (see **page 37**) is universal. They did this by performing a cross-cultural study involving mothers and infants in 3 diverse countries. It was found that mothers in America, China and Germany all exhibited the same behaviour of using a rising tone to indicate to their infants that it was their turn in an interaction between the pair. This supports the idea that caregiverese is an innate, biological device to help promote the formation and maintenance of attachments.

OTHER STUDIES

- Condon & Sander (1974) slowed down infants' movements by analysing frame-by-frame video recordings of their actions to find that they moved in sequence with adults' speech to create a type of turn-taking 'conversation'. This supports the idea of interactional synchrony.

- Melzoff & Moore (1977) reported that 2- to 3-week-old infants tend to imitate adults' specific facial expressions and hand movements. This supports the notion that infant mimicry is an innate ability that helps to form attachments, especially as it was later observed in infants of less than 3 days old.

- Klaus & Kennell (1976) performed a comparison of mothers who had lengthy periods of physical contact with their babies that lasted several hours a day with mothers who only had physical contact with their babies during feeding in the 3 days after birth. They found that mothers with the greater physical contact cuddled their infants more and made greater eye contact with them. The effects were still noticeable a year later, which suggests greater physical contact creates stronger and closer attachment formation.

Description

Interactions between a caregiver and an infant serve to develop and maintain the attachment bond between them. Though an infant cannot talk at this stage of development, meaningful and complex communication between the infant and caregiver does occur in several ways.

- *Interactional synchrony* concerns how infants move their bodies in time with the rhythm of their caregivers' vocal language to create a type of 'turn-taking', as seen in 2-way spoken conversations. This helps to reinforce and maintain the attachment bond between infants and caregivers.

- *Reciprocity* concerns the interactions between caregivers and infants that result in mutual behaviour, where both

Fig 3.1 Interactions between caregivers and infants help to develop and maintain attachment bonds

✔ Klaus & Kennell's (1976) findings that infants who have greater physical contact with their mothers go on to develop stronger and closer attachments is backed up by Chateau & Wiberg (1984), who found the same results with middle-class Swedish mothers.

✔ The study of infant–caregiver interactions has seen the development of innovative research methods, such as analysing video recordings of interactions frame-by-frame as performed by Condon & Sander (1974). This has allowed psychologists to gain an understanding of such interactions and their role in helping form attachments.

✔ Non-verbal forms of communication between infants and caregivers have an evolutionary survival value, as they help a child to be nurtured and protected. Infants can express their needs and have them met. The attachment bond such communications help to create also serves to keep close proximity between infant and caregiver.

individuals motivate responses from each other. This also serves to reinforce and maintain the attachment bond.

- *Bodily contact* concerns the physical interactions between caregivers and infants that help to form the attachment bond, especially in the period immediately after birth.

- *Mimicking* concerns infants' apparent innate ability to imitate their caregivers' facial expressions. This is seen as a biological device to assist in the formation of attachments.

- *Caregiverese* concerns how adults who interact with infants often use a modified form of vocal language that is high-pitched, slow, repetitive and song-like. This assists communication between caregivers and infants and again helps strengthen and maintain attachment bonds.

✖ **Negative evaluation**

✖ Interactional synchrony is not found in all cultures. Le Vine *et al.* (1994) reported that Kenyan mothers have little such interactions with their infants, but form a high amount of secure attachments (see **page 46**). This goes against the idea that interactional synchrony is necessary for healthy attachment development.

✖ Caregiverese is often used by adults with all infants, not just the ones they have an attachment with. Therefore, although it seems to assist communication between adults and children, it is possible that it does not specifically help form attachments.

✖ Infants cannot speak, so interpreting their behaviour is problematic, making it difficult to draw conclusions about infant–caregiver interactions.

Practical application

A practical application that comes from Klaus & Kennell's study is that hospitals now place mothers and babies in the same room after birth (rather than in different rooms, which used to be the case) to encourage the formation of attachments.

pp. 102–4

3 Attachment
Stages of attachment development

Focal study

Schaffer & Emerson (1964) investigated whether there was a common pattern of attachment formation. Sixty newborn infants were studied each month in their own homes, with their mothers, for 12 months. They were studied again at 18 months of age. Interviews were conducted with mothers, and questions were asked about whom infants smiled at, whom they responded to, and who and what caused them distress. Observations were also made on the monthly visits. Most infants began showing separation protest (see **page 48**) from their main caregiver at between 6 and 8 months of age, with stranger anxiety following a month later. Mothers of strongly attached infants responded more quickly to their needs and gave more opportunities for interactions. Most infants developed multiple attachments – at 18 months, 87 per cent had at least 2 attachments and 31 per cent had 5 or more. Infants behaved similarly to different attachment figures. 39 per cent of prime attachments were not to the main caregiver. This suggests there is a common pattern of attachment formation and that attachments are more easily made with those showing sensitive responsiveness. Multiple attachments are the norm and of similar quality.

OTHER STUDIES

- Carpenter (1975) gave infants unfamiliar and familiar voices and faces. Sometimes the face and the voice were of the same person and sometimes not. It was found that 2-week-old babies looked at a face longer when it was their mother's accompanied by her voice and showed distress when it was her face accompanied by a different voice. This suggests that infants can recognise and are attracted to their mothers from an early age, which contradicts Schaffer & Emerson's (1964) finding that infants were initially attracted to anyone who interacted with them.

- Lamb et al. (1982) studied the relationships and attachments that infants had to people like fathers, grandparents and siblings, and found that different attachments served different purposes but were of equal strength. This supports Schaffer & Emerson's finding that multiple attachments are of similar quality.

- Rutter (1981) found that multiple attachments were the norm, supporting Schaffer & Emerson's similar findings.

Description

The development of infants' attachments occurs in 4 universal, distinct stages.

1. The first stage, the *pre-attachment phase*, lasts from birth to 3 months of age. From 6 weeks of age infants become attracted to other humans, preferring them to objects and events. This preference is demonstrated by infants smiling at people's faces.

2. The second stage, the *indiscriminate attachment phase*, lasts from 3 to 7 or 8 months of age. Infants start to discriminate between familiar and unfamiliar people, smiling more at people they know. They still allow strangers to handle and look after them though.

Fig 3.2 Most children develop multiple attachments to other people, such as grandparents

3 The third stage, the *discriminate attachment phase*, lasts from 7 to 8 months onwards. Infants develop specific attachments, staying close to preferred people, showing distress and anxiety when separated from them. They avoid unfamiliar people and protest when strangers handle them.

4 The final stage is the *multiple attachment phase*, occurring from 9 months onwards. Infants develop strong, emotional bonds with other major caregivers, like grandparents, and non-caregivers, like siblings. Fear of strangers weakens, but the prime attachment to the mother figure is still the strongest.

Practical application

The main practical application drawn from research into attachment formation is that to develop strong, secure attachments caregivers should show sensitive responsiveness, recognising and responding appropriately to their infants' needs.

pp. 104–6

3 Attachment
The role of the father

Focal study

Lucassen *et al.* (2011) performed a meta-analysis of 22 studies to investigate the association between the sensitivity of childcare provided by fathers and the security of attachment with their children. The review consisted of studies that used observational measures to measure interaction between fathers and children as well as the Strange Situation procedure (see **page 46**). High levels of paternal sensitivity were found to be associated with higher infant–father attachment security. This suggests that, with fathers as well as with mothers, showing sensitive responsiveness to children's needs leads to more secure attachments with them. Interestingly, fathers' sensitive play combined with stimulation was not more strongly associated with attachment security than sensitive interactions without the stimulation of play, which implies that a father's role as playmate is not that important in developing strong, secure attachments.

OTHER STUDIES

- Hrdy (1999) found that fathers were less able than mothers to detect low levels of infant distress, which supports the idea that males are less suitable attachment figures. However, Lamb (1987) found that when men become main caregivers they quickly develop sensitivity to children's needs, which implies that sensitivity is not limited to just women.

- Bernier & Miljkovitch (2009) found that single-parent fathers develop similar attachments with their children to those that they had with their own fathers. However, this was not found in married fathers, so continuity of attachment seems to occur more where fathers are sole caregivers.

- Belsky et al. (2009) found that fathers with high levels of marital intimacy had more secure attachments with their children. This supports the idea that the emotional closeness of relation-ships between fathers and partners is reflected in the quality of relationships that fathers have with their children.

- Brown et al. (2010) found that high levels of supportive co-parenting (sharing childcare duties) was related to more secure attachment types between fathers and children, but not between mothers and children. This suggests that supportive co-parenting is important for fathers in developing positive relationships with their children.

Description

Traditionally fathers have been seen as minor attachment figures, providing resources, but little childcare. Females were seen as 'natural' caregivers and males were considered to be biologically unsuited to such a role. Some people see fathers not as caregivers, but as a source of exciting, unpredictable, physical play. However, in Britain, in heterosexual partnerships, 10 per cent of main child caregivers are male, while 9 per cent (186,000) of single parents are also male (2013 figures). Research shows that fathers can develop sensitive responsiveness (perceiving and providing appropriate care) when assuming a main caring role. Several important factors have been identified in the relationship between fathers and children:

Fig 3.3 Do children attach to fathers just as playmates, or can the father fulfil a greater role?

✔ Children who have secure attachments with their fathers have good peer relationships, fewer problem behaviours and are more able to control their emotions. This illustrates the positive influence fathers can have on children's development.

✔ Fathers are important for mothers as well as children. Fathers who help with childcare allow mothers to have some time for themselves, which helps reduce stress, increases self-esteem and enables mothers to interact positively with their children.

✔ Children without fathers often do less well at school and show high levels of risk-taking and aggression. This suggests that fathers can help prevent negative developmental outcomes.

- *Degree of sensitivity* – fathers who are sensitive to their children's needs develop more secure attachments with them.
- *Type of attachment with father's own parents* – single-parent fathers tend to develop similar attachment types with their children to those that they had with their own parents.
- *Marital intimacy* – the amount of intimacy (emotional closeness) a father has with his partner is positively correlated with the security of attachment he develops with his children.
- *Supportive co-parenting* – fathers who assist their partners in providing childcare develop stronger, more secure attachments with their children.

✗ Much research evidence concerning father–infant attachments is correlational and does not show causality. For example, there is a relationship between fathers who interact a lot with their children and those children developing secure attachments. But, it might be that more sensitive fathers interact more with their children.

✗ Early interaction with their children is important for fathers in developing positive relationships with them, but few employers encourage male workers to take the paternal leave they are legally entitled to.

✗ Although research shows that men make good main caregivers, society has a long way to catch up. Few nursery and primary school teachers are male and many airlines will not even let men sit next to children.

Practical application

One practical application is in parenting classes. Skills which increase male sensitivity to children's needs can be taught in such classes so that fathers develop more secure relationships with their children. Research evidence could also be used to help break down society's suspicions about men who care for children.

pp. 107–9

3 Attachment
Animal studies of attachment

Focal study

Lorenz (1935) investigated the mechanisms behind imprinting, whereby newborn animals follow the first moving thing they meet. Lorenz split a clutch of goose eggs into 2 batches, 1 of which hatched naturally by the mother and the other hatched in an incubator. Lorenz made sure he was the first moving object the goslings met. He marked each one, so he knew which were naturally hatched and which were incubator hatched. He then placed them all under a box, releasing them simultaneously in the presence of both the mother and himself. Straight after birth, the naturally hatched goslings had followed their mother, while the incubator hatched goslings followed Lorenz. When released from the upturned box, the same behaviour was seen, and these attachments proved to be irreversible. Imprinting only occurred in a 'critical time period' between 4 and 25 hours after hatching. This suggests that imprinting is a form of attachment that helps young creatures keep close proximity to the first moving object they encounter.

Description

A lot of the early research into attachment theory was performed on animals. Indeed most of the theories that were put forward to explain attachment came out of research performed on animals. One of the earliest explanations of attachment behaviour was that of the *learning theory*. This saw attachments as being based on feeding and formed from experience with environmental interactions. Support for behaviourist explanations, such as this, came mostly from animal studies. The major theorist into attachment behaviour was John Bowlby. Although he was originally influenced by Freudian psychodynamic thinking, his classic *monotropic theory of attachment*

OTHER STUDIES

- Harlow (1959) gave baby rhesus monkeys, separated at birth from their mothers, a choice between a harsh wire surrogate mother that provided milk and a soft towelling mother that provided no food. The monkeys preferred the soft towelling mother, using it as a safe base to explore from. This suggests that attachment is based more on emotional security than on feeding.

- Sluckin (1966) performed a variation of Lorenz's study on ducklings. He found that imprinting would still occur after ducklings had been isolated for 5 days – beyond the established critical time period. This suggests that the critical period is actually a 'sensitive' (best) period, beyond which imprinting, though more difficult, can still be achieved.

- Harlow et al. (1965) found that newborn monkeys raised in total isolation showed signs of psychological disturbance. The females made very poor mothers, some even killing their babies. This suggests social interactions are essential for normal development.

Fig 3.4 Whooping cranes and their imprinted micro-light aircraft parents

✔ The shocking results of Harlow et al.'s (1965) study were found to be reversible by Harlow & Suomi (1972). They placed isolated monkeys with an opposite sex younger 'therapist' monkey, gradually increasing contact time. By 3 years of age they had totally recovered.

✔ The use of animal research enabled psychologists to study attachment behaviour in ways that would not have been practically or ethically possible with human participants.

✔ The results of animal studies enabled psychologists to realise that attachment theories based on feeding were wrong. They led to the much better considered theories of Bowlby that saw attachment as a biological device centred on its survival value.

(see **page 45**), which explains how attachments are formed and maintained, and his *maternal deprivation hypothesis* (see **page 48**), which explains what happens when attachments are broken, were formed from animal studies. The work of Konrad Lorenz centred on the idea of *imprinting* that saw animals following the first large moving object they encountered. Bowlby came to see attachment as a human form of imprinting. Harry Harlow's work with rhesus monkeys was also important. Harlow showed, in studies involving separating baby monkeys from their mothers, that behaviourist explanations were wrong and that attachment appeared to be based more on emotional security than feeding.

✖ Negative evaluation

✖ The problem with animal studies is *generalisation*: what is true for animals is not necessarily true for humans. Imprinting only occurs in nidifugous birds (ones that leave the nest early), so imprinting behaviour is not representative of most bird species (non-nidifugous species), let alone humans.

✖ There are ethical issues of harm with animal studies, like those of Harlow where many of the monkeys died. Harlow even invented a 'rape rack', a device to which female monkeys were tied and forcibly mated.

✖ Lorenz's membership of the Nazi party has led to accusations that his belief in genetically inherited characteristics contaminated his work with researcher bias.

Practical application

Imprinting research has helped reintroduce migratory birds to areas where they have become extinct. Whooping cranes are imprinted onto micro-light aircraft and taught the traditional migratory flight paths. Farmers also use imprinting by putting an orphaned lamb wearing the skin of a dead lamb with the dead lamb's mother so that she will accept it.

pp. 109–14

3 Attachment
Explanations of attachment

Focal study

Fox (1977) investigated learning theory's central belief that attachments occur due to feeding from the main caregiver. The participants were 122 children who were born and raised on Israeli kibbutzim (collective farms). Due to their parents' working commitments, the majority of the children's caregiving, including feeding, was provided by *metapelets* (specialist child caregivers). Care was provided by the metapelets in specialist children's centres, with some children returning to their parents in the evenings and others only at weekends. Separation and reunion behaviours with both metapelets and mothers were observed and recorded. It was found that although children protested equally to either mother or metapelet separation when left with a stranger, generally children were more attached to their mothers. Some children showed little if any attachment to their metapelets. As metapelets did most of the feeding, these findings go against the learning theory.

Description

Explanations of attachments give reasons as to why and how attachments form.

Learning theory is a behaviourist explanation that sees attachments as developing through conditioning processes, where an infant learns to associate a caregiver with feeding. With *classical conditioning* the stimulus of food, which produces a natural response of pleasure, is paired with the stimulus of a caregiver, until the caregiver alone produces the pleasure response. With *operant conditioning* caregivers are a source of *negative reinforcement* (escaping something unpleasant), as they become associated with removing the unpleasant sensation of hunger.

OTHER STUDIES

- Dollard & Miller (1950) calculated that babies are fed over 2,000 times by their mothers in the first year of life, thus presenting ample opportunities for attachments to form via association, in line with learning theory.

- Schaffer & Emerson (1964) (see **page 38**) found that in 39 per cent of cases, the mother, who was usually the main caregiver and feeder, was not a baby's main attachment figure. This goes against learning theory, as it suggests that attachments are often made not for reasons of food.

- Rutter (1981) found that infants display a whole range of attachment behaviours towards a variety of attachment figures, not just mothers. Indeed there is no particular attachment behaviour used specifically and exclusively for mothers. This lowers support for Bowlby's theory of monotropy (that infants form one prime attachment to a mother-figure).

Fig 3.5 Learning theory sees attachments as forming due to an association being developed between mother and feeding

✔ Although not generally supported by research evidence, learning theory did stimulate a lot of interest in attachment theory and research into it eventually led to Bowlby's more favoured theory.

✔ There is plenty of evidence to support many aspects of Bowlby's theory, for instance the *continuity hypothesis*, where later relationships are seen to reflect early attachment types. Research has shown that the quality of early attachment patterns is indeed reflected in later romantic relationships.

✔ Bowlby's theory puts attachment behaviour into an evolutionary perspective, showing how attachments have developed through natural selection. Those who demonstrated such behaviour had an adaptive advantage to survive to maturity, reproduce and pass on the genes for attachment behaviour to their children. Thus the behaviour became more widespread throughout the population.

Bowlby's *monotropic theory* is an evolutionary explanation of attachment. It sees infants as having an innate tendency to form a bond with one prime attachment figure, which brings with it a survival value through keeping close proximity to that attachment figure. Infants have *social releasers* (innate social behaviours), such as crying, smiling, vocalising and following behaviours, which stimulate adult caregiving. These behaviours become focused on the adult giving the most sensitive care. Bowlby believed there was a *critical period*, a specific time period within which this attachment must form, else it never would. Bowlby saw the monotropic attachment (to one person) as forming an *internal working model*, a blueprint for all future relationships.

✖ Negative evaluation

✖ Schaffer (1971) argued that learning theory puts things the wrong way round: babies do not 'live to eat', but 'eat to live'. Therefore they are active seekers of stimulation, not passive recipients of nutrition.

✖ Learning theory, via conditioning, explains the acquisition of simple behaviours, but not more complex behaviours like attachment, which has an intense emotional component.

✖ Bowlby sees attachments as forming due to mere exposure of infants to caregivers. However, Schaffer & Emerson's (1964) study showed that attachments form with those adults who display the most *sensitive responsiveness*, identifying and responding appropriately to an infant's needs. This suggests that attachment formation is a more dynamic process than Bowlby claimed.

Practical application

A practical application of Bowlby's theory is that parents should receive parenting classes that emphasise the importance of sensitive responsiveness in developing secure attachments – important not just immediately, but also in developing successful romantic relationships in later life.

pp. 115–19

3 Attachment

Ainsworth's 'Strange Situation'

Focal study

Ainsworth *et al.* (1978) tested 106 young infants between 9 and 18 months old under conditions of mild stress and novelty, to assess *stranger anxiety, separation anxiety* and the *secure base concept*. The Strange Situation procedure involved an 81 square foot (about 7.5 square metre) novel environment divided into 16 squares, which was used to track movements and consisted of 8 episodes involving mothers and strangers in various scenarios of arrival and departure. Five categories were recorded: *proximity and contact-seeking behaviours, contact-maintaining behaviours, proximity and interaction-avoiding behaviours, contact and interaction-resisting behaviours* and *search behaviours*. Every 5 seconds the category of behaviour was recorded and assessed on a scale of 1–7. 15 per cent of infants were *insecure-avoidant* attachment type, 15 per cent were *insecure-resistant* and 70 per cent were *securely attached*. Ainsworth concluded that *sensitive responsiveness* was the key factor, as sensitive caregivers are accepting, co-operative and accessible, attending appropriately to their infant's needs. Sensitive mothers tend to have securely attached infants.

Description

Following on from her earlier work with mothers and babies in Uganda and Baltimore, Ainsworth created the *Strange Situation*, a controlled observation of a mother and stranger leaving and returning to a room where an infant is playing. Three types of attachment were observed:

1 *Securely attached* (Type B), where children are willing to explore, have high stranger anxiety, are easy to soothe and are enthusiastic at their caregiver's return. Caregivers are sensitive to their infants' needs.

2 *Insecure-avoidant* (Type A), where children are willing to explore, have low stranger anxiety, are indifferent to separation and avoid contact at the

OTHER STUDIES

- Van Ijzendoorn & Kroonenberg (1988) performed a meta-analysis of 32 Strange Situation studies from 8 countries. They found Type A = 21 per cent, Type B = 67 per cent and Type C = 12 per cent, so generally the results were similar to Ainsworth's. However, there were some differences in attachment types in some cultures, reflecting differences in childrearing practices. Greater intra-cultural differences were found that reflected socio-economic differences within a culture. Overall, Type B was dominant in all cultures, which suggests some degree of biological origin to attachment types.

- Main & Solomon (1986) found a fourth attachment type, *insecure-disorganised* (Type D), a rare type where children display a confusing mix of approach and avoidance behaviours. Ainsworth agreed with the existence of this type.

- McMahon-True *et al.* (2001) found no existence of Type A in the Dogon people of Mali, due to their natural childrearing practices. This suggests the Strange Situation is not suitable for all cultures.

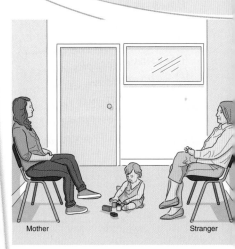

Mother   Stranger

Fig 3.6 The Strange Situation is a procedure for measuring the strength and type of infants' attachments to their mothers

✔ The Strange Situation became a *paradigm* study, the accepted method of assessing attachment behaviour, and has been used in countless studies.

✔ The Strange Situation is accused of being unethical, as it subjects infants to stress. But it is modelled on everyday experiences where mothers do leave children for brief periods in different settings and with strangers, for example babysitters.

✔ Van Ijzendoorn & Schuengel (1999) see Ainsworth's studies as important, as her central finding of parental sensitivity being linked to the quality of attachment has been widely replicated by others using larger samples. This is true also in cross-cultural studies.

return of their caregiver.
Caregivers ignore their infants.

3 *Insecure-resistant* (Type C), where children are unwilling to explore, have high stranger anxiety, are distressed at separation and seek and reject contact at the return of caregivers. Caregivers show simultaneous opposite feelings and behaviour towards their infants.

Differences have been found in patterns of attachment types in replications of the Strange Situation in other cultures, such as that by Van Ijzendoorn & Kroonenberg (1988), though generally results were similar to what Ainsworth found. Indeed intra-cultural differences (differences between sub-cultural groupings within a culture) were often greater than inter-cultural differences (differences between different cultures).

❌ Negative evaluation

✗ Improper use of the Strange Situation has serious implications. Yeo (2003) reported how judgements are made about whether Aboriginal children should be in care, based on what white Australian culture deems appropriate parenting, leading to 25 per cent of children in care being Aborigines.

✗ The Strange Situation is not a valid measure of attachment, as the technique only measures attachment type to one attachment figure. Main & Weston (1981) found that children acted differently in the Strange Situation depending on which parent they were with.

✗ As attachment types vary cross-culturally and the Strange Situation is not applicable to all cultures, attachment theory is *culture bound* and appropriate mainly to Western cultures.

Practical application
The Strange Situation is used to make informed decisions about child placements in such instances as fostering – for example, to assess what children's attachment needs are when being placed in care and to determine whether or not children should be removed from their home environment.

AQA
AQA
A-level

Psychology
For A-level Year 1 and AS
1

Jean-Marc Lawton
Eleanor Willard

pp. 119–28

3 Attachment

Bowlby's maternal deprivation hypothesis (MDH) (1951)

Focal study

Rutter *et al.* (1998) investigated whether sensitive care could overturn the effects of privation suffered in Romanian orphanages. Three groups of children were studied: orphans adopted before 6 months of age, orphans adopted between 6 months and 2 years of age, and orphans adopted after 2 years of age. A control group of 52 British adopted children were also assessed (to see if negative effects were due to separation from caregivers or institutional conditions). The children's level of cognitive functioning was measured. It was found that 50 per cent of Romanian orphans were cognitively retarded and underweight at initial assessment, while the children in the control group were not. At 4 years of age the orphans showed great improvements in physical and cognitive development, especially those adopted before 6 months of age, who did as well as the British adopted children. This suggests that negative effects of institutionalisation can be overcome with sensitive care.

OTHER STUDIES

- Robertson & Robertson (1971) found that children did show the short-term separation effects predicted by Bowlby's PDD model, but that such effects were preventable if alternative sensitive care and a normal home routine were provided. This suggests that Bowlby is wrong, as attachment disruption effects are not inevitable.

- Hetherington & Stanley-Hagan (1999) found that 25 per cent of children had long-term adjustment problems after parental divorce but most eventually adapted. This suggests that the effects of long-term separation are reversible.

- Schaffer (1996) found that nearly all children are negatively affected by divorce in the short term, which suggests that the effects of long-term deprivation are universal.

- Freud & Dann (1951) reported on 6 orphans, rescued from a Nazi concentration camp, suffering from privation. They had little language, refused to be separated and displayed hostility to adults. They gradually formed attachments with their caregivers, developing rapidly both physically and intellectually. Follow-up studies suggested their recovery was full and permanent.

Description

Bowlby's maternal deprivation hypothesis (MDH) argues that if attachments are broken, even in the short term, serious, permanent damage will occur to children's emotional, social and cognitive development. The MDH is examined by assessing the effects on children of various forms of disruption.

- *Separation* consists of short-term attachment disruption, like being left with a babysitter. The distress is characterised by Bowlby's PDD model (protest, despair, detachment). However, later research shows that such effects are avoidable if alternative, sensitive care is provided.

- *Deprivation* consists of long-term attachment disruption, such as through divorce. Effects are more

Fig 3.7 Professor Rutter's studies of Romanian orphans have aimed to see if the effects of institutionalisation can be overcome through loving care by adoptive parents

✔ It would seem logical that long-term separation would have greater negative effects on children's development than short-term separation, and research evidence backs this up.

✔ Robertson & Robertson's work detailing the effects of children undergoing short-term separations led to radical changes in hospital care. Regular visiting by family members was introduced, and work shifts were arranged so that children had consistent contact with familiar nurses in order for alternative attachments to form and negative separation effects to be avoided.

✔ Morison & Elwood (2005) found similar results to Rutter with a group of Romanian orphans adopted in Canada, which suggests Rutter's findings are reliable.

severe and longer lasting, but most children recover over time.

● *Privation* involves never forming attachments, with severe developmental retardation occurring. However, such effects are generally reversible in the long term if sensitive care is provided.

● *Institutionalisation* concerns childcare, such as that provided by children's homes. The effects resemble those of deprivation and privation. *Romanian orphanage studies* have shown that such negative effects can again be overcome by the provision of sensitive, nurturing care.

Overall, Bowlby's MDH can be seen to be valid in terms of the negative effects it details as a result of attachment disruption. However, contrary to Bowlby's beliefs, most negative effects seem to be avoidable or reversible.

✘ Negative evaluation

✘ Most evidence linking short-term separation to negative outcomes is correlational and does not show causality. Other factors may be involved; indeed Kagan *et al.* (1978) found no direct causal link between separation and later emotional and behavioural difficulties.

✘ Divorce can be beneficial to children, as it removes the negative environment of marital conflict and allows parents to have more time to give sensitive care to their children, meaning development actually improves in the long term rather than worsens.

✘ As the Romanian orphans were not studied during their time within the Romanian orphanages, it is not possible to state which aspects of their privation were most damaging to their development.

Practical application
A practical application of research into long-term deprivation is that some American states legally require divorcing parents to attend educational classes that teach them to understand and avoid the difficulties associated with disrupted attachments.

pp. 129–37

3 Attachment

The influence of early attachment on childhood and adult relationships

Focal study

Hazan & Shaver (1987) assessed possible links between childhood attachment and adult romantic relationships. 620 heterosexual participants responded to a 'love quiz' in a newspaper, selecting which of 3 descriptions – a secure, an insecure-resistant or an insecure-avoidant attachment type – reflected their feelings of adult romance. Participants also completed a checklist relating to childhood relationships with parents. The percentages of adults in the different attachment types matched those in Ainsworth's Strange Situation. Those identified with childhood secure attachments had positive perceptions of adult relationships and longer-lasting relationships. Those with insecure-resistant attachments doubted the existence of romantic love and its essentialness to happiness. Those with insecure-avoidant attachments had more self-doubts and, as in those with insecure attachments, increased loneliness. It was concluded that childhood attachment types are positively correlated with childhood attachment experiences.

Description

Bowlby's *continuity hypothesis* sees children's attachment types reflected in later relationships. This is based on the *internal working model*, which perceives an infant's main attachment relationship as forming a blueprint for future relationships. Attachment style is seen as providing children with beliefs about themselves and others and about the nature of relationships. According to this model, attachment types predict adult relationships, so that those with secure attachments in childhood go on to have intimate, secure adult relationships, while those with insecure attachments do not. Hazan & Shaver (1987) additionally proposed that early attachment patterns affect *romantic relationships*, *caregiving* and *sexuality* in adulthood.

OTHER STUDIES

- McCarthy (1999) assessed women with childhood insecure attachments. He found that women with insecure-avoidant attachments had less successful adult romantic relations, while those with insecure-resistant attachments had problems forming non-romantic adult friendships. This supports Bowlby's idea of an internal working model.

- Brennan & Shaver (1995) found that participants with insecure-avoidant attachments would have sex without strong feelings of love or being in a long-lasting relationship. Hazan & Shaver (1994) found that such individuals were more likely to have one-night stands and casual sex outside of established relationships and also preferred purely sexual contact to emotional contact. These studies support the concept of the internal working model.

- Kirkpatrick & Davis (1994) studied 300 dating couples for 3 years and found that participants with secure childhood attachments were more likely to have secure, satisfying relations. This supports Bowlby's continuity hypothesis.

Fig 3.8 Research suggests that individuals who form secure infant attachments go on to enjoy loving, long-lasting adult relationships

Research indicates that continuity between early attachment styles and the quality of childhood relationships exists. Evidence also suggests that children who form attachments to each other in early life do not form romantic, sexual relationships with each other in adulthood. The idea of continuity between adults' attachment types and their children's is supported, possibly indicating a social learning effect. The quality of later adult relationships is related to early attachment styles, though it is not inevitable that those with insecure attachments as children will be condemned to unsuccessful relationships as adults. Individuals with insecure attachments as children can develop secure adult relationships if they are in relationships with those with secure attachments.

Practical application

The main practical application of research into this area is in relationship counselling. Attention needs to be paid to attachment styles of partners, in order for the best strategies to be formed to successfully guide individuals through times of relationship stress.

pp. 138–43

4 Approaches

The behaviourist approach

Focal study

Pavlov (1903), investigating the role of salivation in digestion, became interested in how dogs learned to salivate before food was presented to them. The dogs had learned to predict the arrival of food by making associations, such as the kitchen door being opened, with being fed. The stimulus of food (unconditioned stimulus – UCS) naturally produced the response of salivation (unconditioned response – UCR), but Pavlov also rang a bell (conditioned stimulus – CS) when presenting the food, something that does not naturally produce the response of salivation. After doing this an average of 7 times, a dog would then salivate just to the sound of the bell (conditioned response – CR) with no presentation of food. This suggests that the dogs had learned to associate the bell with the presentation of food. Pavlov called this kind of learning classical conditioning.

OTHER STUDIES

- Skinner (1948) found that rats, placed in a Skinner box, would move around and sometimes accidentally knock a lever, triggering the release of a food pellet. Gradually the rats came to associate pressing the lever with getting rewarded with food, and eventually they did this immediately and consistently upon being put in the box. This suggests the food pellet was acting as a positive reinforcement, strengthening the behaviour and increasing the chances that it would occur again in similar circumstances.
- Bandura *et al.* (1961) found that children who observed an adult model behave aggressively by beating a 'Bobo doll' were more aggressive when allowed to play with toys than children who observed a non-aggressive adult model or no model at all. Boys tended to imitate a model more if the model was male, while girls tended to imitate a model more if the model was female. This suggests that behaviour can be learned through observation and imitation of a role model, especially when an individual identifies with a model.

Description

The behaviourist approach sees humans born as *tabula rasa* ('blank slates') with all behaviour learned from experience and no genetic influences. The approach only focuses on observable behaviours, as they are seen as scientifically measurable. Therefore, there is no place in behaviourism for the study of hidden mental processes. Behaviourism believes it is valid to study animals, as they share similar principles of learning with humans. There are 3 main forms of learning:

1 *Classical conditioning*, investigated by *Pavlov*, concerns reflex actions, where a stimulus becomes associated with a response and as such occurs when a response produced naturally by a specific stimulus becomes associated with another stimulus not normally associated with that response.

2 *Operant conditioning*, investigated by *Skinner*, concerns voluntary behaviour, with learning occurring via reinforcement of

Before learning

Food (UCS) → *Salivation* (UCR)

During learning

Food (UCS) + *Bell* (CS) → *Salivation* (UCR)

After learning

Bell (CS) → *Salivation* (CR)

Fig 4.1 Classical conditioning as produced by Pavlov's dogs

behaviour. This may be through *positive reinforcement*, where a behaviour becomes likely to occur again because it had a pleasant outcome, or through *negative reinforcement*, where a behaviour becomes likely to occur again because it resulted in avoidance of something unpleasant happening.

3 *Social learning theory*, investigated by *Bandura*, involves behaviour being learned through observation and imitation of models whose behaviours are seen to be reinforced. *Identification* concerns when an individual is influenced by another because they are likeable or similar to them. *Vicarious reinforcement* concerns the rewards an observer sees another receiving for their behaviour. The types of consideration (thinking) that occur before an observed behaviour is imitated are known as *mediational processes*.

Negative evaluation

✘ Critics see behaviourism as being far too rooted in the results from animal research. Animals do not necessarily learn in the same way as humans, which creates problems of generalising research findings from animals to humans.

✘ Behaviourism sees behaviour as deterministic, whereby experience programmes us to act unthinkingly in certain ways. There is no role for free will, whereby individuals consciously decide on their behaviour.

✘ Behaviourism tends to ignore the important role that nature plays in determining behaviour. The approach sees all behaviour as learned, therefore neglecting the influence of factors such as genetics and evolution in shaping behaviour.

Practical application

One practical application of the approach is behavioural treatments for mental disorders. An example of this is **systematic desensitisation** (see **page 73**), which is used to treat phobias by using relaxation strategies to break down irrational fears in a step-by-step approach.

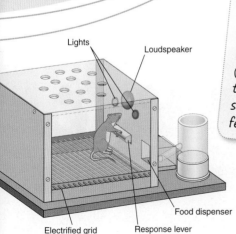

Lights
Loudspeaker
Food dispenser
Electrified grid
Response lever

Fig 4.2 Skinner's box for rats

AQA A-level Psychology For A-level Year 1 and AS

pp. 206–17

4 Approaches
The origins of psychology and the cognitive approach

Focal study

Simons & Chabris (1999) investigated to what extent people are aware of information present in their visual field. 228 participants watched films of 2 teams of 3 players, one team dressed in white T-shirts and the other in black T-shirts, passing a basketball to team members. Participants were specifically asked to count the number of passes made by the white team. After doing this, participants were asked if they had noticed anything unusual. 54 per cent failed to notice a man in a gorilla suit or a woman with an umbrella who were prominent in the films. This suggests that humans are only aware of information in their visual field that they select to pay attention to. The study also illustrates how scientific means of investigation can be used to explore the role of mental processes in behaviour.

Description

Wundt (1875) established the first psychology laboratory in Leipzig, Germany, using *introspection* as his research tool, whereby researchers examined their own conscious thoughts, feelings and sensations in a controlled environment. However, findings proved not to be replicable, as they were based on only one person's subjective viewpoint. Introspection was soon abandoned, but it was from this starting point that psychology developed to use increasingly scientific methods. Although not all aspects of modern psychology are totally scientific, nor are all psychologists scientists, the majority of the subject and its practitioners are seen as scientifically based.

Neisser (1959) is credited with starting *cognitive psychology*. Although a more modern approach, cognitive psychology has links with introspection, as both see behaviour as being understood by reference to the mental processes

OTHER STUDIES

- Postman & Bruner (1947) showed participants a photo of a black man and a white man arguing, with the white man brandishing a knife. When asked to recall the photo, many participants wrongly recalled the black man having the knife. This illustrates how schema affect mental processes such perception, as the stereotype of black people being aggressive and carrying weapons was a common view held at the time.

- Hemond *et al.* (2007) gave participants pictures of faces and objects to look at while simultaneously scanning their brains with an fMRI scanner. It was found that the *fusiform gyrus* brain area was activated significantly more during face recognition than during object recognition, which suggests this brain area is associated with processing faces. This demonstrates how the cognitive and biological approaches can be combined together to investigate mental processes.

Fig 4.3 Simons & Chabris found that many observers did not notice a man in a gorilla suit. Figure provided by Daniel Simons.

- ✔ Cognitive psychology has been successfully combined with the biological approach of neuroscience to create *cognitive neuroscience*. The approach uses scientific experimentation and scanning techniques to investigate where in the brain different mental processes are based.
- ✔ Because cognitive psychology tends to use experimental methods, its research can be seen to have scientific rigour. For example, research is easily replicable to test the validity of findings.
- ✔ The cognitive approach can be considered as superior to behaviourism. This is because it sees behaviour as understood through reference to the mental processes occurring between stimuli and responses and not just the stimuli and responses themselves.

underpinning it. The approach has 4 assumptions:

1 *Scientific study* – mental processes should be investigated through scientifically based studies.

2 *Mind as a computer* – the mind can be seen as similar to a computer in having an input of sensory information, which is then processed to produce an output in the form of behaviour.

3 *Importance of mental processes* – the role of stimulus and response in behaviour can only be truly understood by reference to the mental processes occurring between them.

4 *The role of schemas* – behaviour is affected by schemas, mental representations of the world formed from experience, which affect how individuals perceive the world. Ultimately an individual will perceive what they expect to perceive based on previous experience.

❌ **Negative evaluation**

- ✘ The strong emphasis on laboratory experiments means that research can often lack external validity, as the mental processes assessed are often not investigated in everyday situations and contexts.
- ✘ The perception of the human mind as working similarly to a computer is criticised as being over-mechanistic. Humans have strong elements of free will in their thinking and behaviour, which arguably computers do not have.
- ✘ The cognitive approach has been accused of failing to properly consider the important role of emotion in determining human behaviour.

Practical application

Findings from research into mental processes have produced practical applications, such as devising strategies for people with impairments to their working memory to help them focus better on tasks at hand. Examples include breaking instructions down into individual steps and getting sufferers to periodically repeat these instructions.

pp. 198, 218–23

4 Approaches
The biological approach

Focal study

Grootheest *et al.* (2005) investigated the extent to which obsessive–compulsive disorder (OCD) is an inherited condition. A meta-analysis of 28 twin studies, ranging from 1929 to the modern era (though the vast majority were carried out since 1965 under modern diagnostic criteria), was conducted. It comprised 10,034 twin pairs. It was found that OCD seemed to have a genetic component ranging from 45 to 65 per cent in children and from 27 to 47 per cent in adults. This strongly suggests that OCD has a genetic basis, especially childhood forms of the disorder. The use of twin studies demonstrates how biology, in this instance in the form of genetics, can have a dominant influence on behaviour.

Description

The *biological approach* sees behaviour as based within the physiology of the body, with *genes, evolution, brain structures* and *biochemistry* being the main influences. The chromosomes inherited from our parents form our *genotype* (our basic genetic make-up) and this interacts with environmental factors to form our *phenotype* (our actual behaviour and characteristics shown). The gradual process of behavioural change that occurs due to the *evolutionary* process of *natural selection* is genetically transmitted and so is also included within the biological approach. *Brain structures* are also seen as important in determining and monitoring behaviour, with different brain areas associated with different types of behavioural functioning. Specific *biological structures* within the

OTHER STUDIES

- Kessler *et al.* (2003) used PET and MRI scans to find that people with schizophrenia had elevated levels of the neurotransmitter dopamine in the basal forebrain and substantia nigra/ventral tegemental brain areas, which illustrates how biochemistry can affect behaviour, on this occasion in the form of a mental disorder.

- Dudley *et al.* (2008) found that ants in salt-poor environments preferred salty solutions to sweet ones, which suggests that this is an adaptive response to maintain evolutionary fitness (salt being essential to survival). This was supported by carnivorous ants not showing the salt preference, as they get ample salt from their prey, and therefore showed how evolution can shape behaviour.

- Siegel & Victoroff (2009) found that defensive and predatory forms of aggression appear to be controlled by the limbic system in the brain, with the cerebral cortex brain area playing an important role in moderating levels of aggression. This illustrates how brain areas are related to specific forms of behaviour in line with the biological approach.

Fig 4.4 Research with identical twins is useful for investigating the basis of certain behaviours

- ✔ The biological approach uses scientific methods of investigation that incorporate measures which are mainly objective (not a researcher's personal opinions). Examples include brain scanning, like MRI and PET scans, and measurements of biochemistry, like dopamine levels.
- ✔ It is possible to combine the biological and cognitive approaches together, as in cognitive neuroscience, to give a fuller understanding of human behaviour. Cognitive neuroscience uses biological techniques, like brain scanning, to try and identify in which particular brain areas specific mental processes are located and managed.
- ✔ The biological approach is supported by a wealth of research evidence that suggests much human behaviour has large biological elements.

body connect together to determine behaviour, such as the 2 parts of the nervous system, the *central nervous system* (CNS) (consisting of the brain and spinal cord), which transmits information to and from the environment, and the *peripheral nervous system* (PNS) (the accompanying system running throughout the body that acts with the CNS), which transmits information concerning the limbs and torso. *Neurons* are the individual nerve cells that transmit information within the nervous system, with each individual possessing billions of them.
The *biochemistry* of the body consists of chemical messengers within the body. *Hormones* are chemical messengers that travel in blood and other bodily fluids, while *neurotransmitters* are chemicals that travel within the brain in cerebral fluid.

✖ Negative evaluation

- ✖ Critics argue that explanations based on the biological approach are too simplistic and do not acknowledge the complexity of a lot of human behaviour. This means that such explanations are *reductionist* (explaining a complex phenomenon in terms of its basic parts) in nature, often failing to appreciate the important role of environment in determining behaviour. Social factors, like childhood experiences and the influence of family and friends, are ignored.
- ✖ The biological approach is better at explaining behaviours which are mainly biologically determined, like Alzheimer's disease, than those which are not so biologically determined, like emotional experiences.
- ✖ Biological therapies often treat the effects of, rather than the causes of, mental disorders. This lowers support for the argument that such disorders are biologically determined.

Practical application

The biological approach has led to many effective treatments for mental disorders, such as drug treatments for depression and schizophrenia, which are by far the most common treatments. There is also electroconvulsive therapy (ECT), which is used to treat severe cases of depression and treatment-resistant schizophrenia.

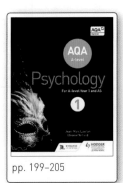

pp. 199–205

5 Biopsychology
The nervous system and neurons

The divisions of the nervous system

The nervous system divides into the *central nervous system* (CNS) and the *peripheral nervous system* (PNS). It provides the biological basis to an individual's psychological experiences.

The CNS

The CNS comprises the *brain* and *spinal cord* and is concerned with maintaining life functions and psychological processes.
- There are many different brain areas with differing functions. Some brain areas are seen as primitive and involved in basic functioning to maintain life, while other areas are more complex and involved with higher level functioning such as thinking and decision making.
- The function of the spinal cord is to facilitate the transfer of information to and from the brain to the PNS.

The PNS

The PNS conveys information to and from the CNS and in essence is the messaging service for the limbs and torso. It sub-divides into 2 divisions: the *somatic nervous system* (SNS) and the *autonomic nervous system* (ANS).
- The SNS mainly transmits and receives information from the senses, such as auditory information from the ears. It also directs muscles to react and move.
- The ANS helps to transmit and receive information from bodily organs, such as the stomach, and divides into 2 further sub-systems: the **sympathetic nervous system**, which generally helps to increase bodily activities, and the **parasympathetic nervous system**, which generally conserves bodily activities by maintaining or decreasing activity.

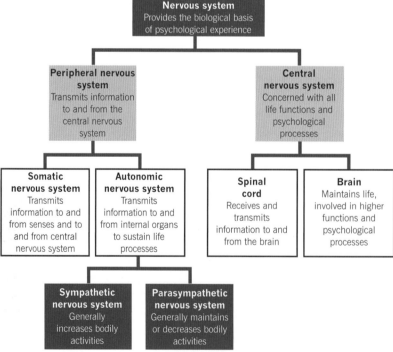

Fig 5.1 Divisions of the nervous system, with an indication of the function of each division

The structure and function of sensory, relay and motor neurons

Neurons are cells that transmit nerve impulses around the nervous system, acting as a kind of bodily communication system. There are about 100 billion neurons in the brain and 1 billion in the spinal cord. There are 3 main types of neurons: *sensory*, *relay* and *motor*, each having a different specialised role to play. The structure of all neurons is generally the same, though there are structural differences in size relating to their function – for instance, motor neurons tend to be longer than other neurons. In all neurons the *dendrite/receptor cell* receives the signal, which then travels through the neuron to the *pre-synaptic terminal*.

- *Sensory neurons* inform the brain about a person's external and internal environment by processing sensory information received by the sensory organs. As sensory neurons only transmit information, they are known as *unipolar* neurons, while *relay* and *motor* neurons are *bipolar*, as they send and receive information.
- *Relay neurons* transmit information from one area of the CNS to another. Relay neurons also connect motor and sensory neurons together.
- *Motor neurons* transmit information from the CNS to help the functioning of bodily organs (including glands – important for the endocrine system) and muscles.

The process of synaptic transmission

Synaptic transmission is the process by which nerve impulses are carried across *synapses* (small gaps between neurons). The nerve impulses transmitted through neurons are electrical in nature and are transmitted across synapses by chemicals called *neurotransmitters*. Initially a nerve impulse travels down a neuron and initiates release of neurotransmitters (brain chemicals) at the *pre-synaptic terminal*. The neurotransmitters are then released into the synaptic fluid within the synapse. The adjoining neuron takes up the neurotransmitters from the synaptic fluid and converts them to an electrical impulse, which travels down the neuron to the next pre-synaptic terminal, and so on.

Not all signals prompt activation in the same way. How this occurs is dependent on the *action potential* of the post-synaptic neuron and the type of information received.

- *Excitatory potentials* act like the accelerator pedal in a car, as they make it more likely to cause the post-synaptic neuron to fire. When this occurs it is known as an *excitatory synapse*.
- *Inhibitory potentials* act like the brake on a car, as they make it less likely for the neuron to fire, and when this occurs and the signal is stopped at the post-synaptic neuron it is known as an *inhibitory synapse*.

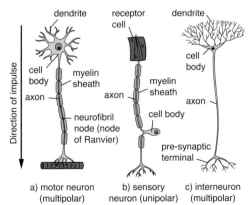

a) motor neuron (multipolar) b) sensory neuron (unipolar) c) interneuron (multipolar)

Fig 5.2 The anatomical differences between neurons

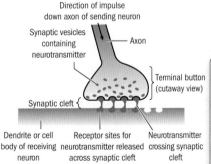

Fig 5.3 A typical synapse between 2 neurons. The nerve impulse travels from the pre-synaptic neuron, across the synaptic cleft, to the post-synaptic neuron

pp. 226–30

5 Biopsychology
The influence of biochemistry on behaviour

The function of the endocrine system

The nervous system receives and sends information around the body using electrical and chemical means (see **page 58**). Another bodily messaging system is the *endocrine system*, a series of glands found throughout the body that release chemicals known as *hormones* via blood and other bodily fluids. This allows information to be sent to the organs of the body in order to affect their behaviour, rather like neurons do in the nervous system.

There are a number of specialist glands in the endocrine system. Each of these, when stimulated, releases particular hormones that produce specific behavioural effects. The *pituitary gland* is located behind the bridge of the nose and to the base of the brain just below the hypothalamus brain area (to which it is attached via nerve fibres). It is a pea-sized structure known as the 'master gland', due to its important role within the endocrine system in regulating the functions of other glands – such as the *ovaries* in females, the *testes* in males and the *thyroid* and *adrenal* glands – and the hormones they secrete.

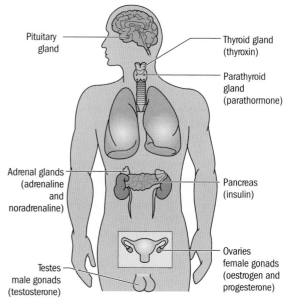

Pituitary gland

Thyroid gland (thyroxin)

Parathyroid gland (parathormone)

Adrenal glands (adrenaline and noradrenaline)

Pancreas (insulin)

Testes male gonads (testosterone)

Ovaries female gonads (oestrogen and progesterone)

Fig 5.4 The endocrine system, showing the major glands in the human body

The pituitary gland

The pituitary gland has 2 lobes (parts): a front part known as the *anterior pituitary* and a back part known as the *posterior pituitary*. The anterior pituitary releases several important hormones: growth hormone, gonadotrophins (puberty hormones), thyroid-stimulating hormone and adrenocorticotrophic hormone (ACTH), which stimulates the adrenal stress hormone cortisol. The posterior pituitary releases the fluid-balance hormone ADH (anti-diuretic hormone).

To activate the pituitary gland the hypothalamus signals to it to either stimulate or inhibit hormone production. The anterior lobe releases hormones on receiving releasing or inhibiting hormones from the hypothalamus. These hypothalamic hormones inform the anterior lobe whether to release more of a specific hormone or cease its release. The hormones of the pituitary gland send signals to other endocrine glands to stimulate or inhibit their own hormone production. For instance, the anterior pituitary lobe will release ACTH to stimulate cortisol production from the adrenal glands (situated near the kidneys) when an individual is stressed. The adrenal glands are an important component of the *fight-or-flight response* (see below) as they facilitate the release of *adrenaline*.

Another important hormone that increasingly interests psychologists is *oxytocin*, which is released from the posterior lobe of the pituitary gland and is secreted during pleasurable activities like playing, cuddling or having sex. Oxytocin is especially important for females, as it causes contractions during labour and also causes the release of milk during breastfeeding. It is important in both males and females in creating bonds between individuals.

The *fight-or-flight response* is generated from the *sympathetic nervous system* branch of the *autonomic nervous system* (ANS) (see **page 58**). It is an innate reflex action (that is, one that requires no conscious thought) that has an evolutionary survival value in helping protect an individual confronted by potentially dangerous situations. The response is activated in times of stress when something is perceived to be a threat to safety, and helps an individual to react more quickly than usual, as well as optimising functioning so the body is able to effectively fight or run away from the threat.

The response can be broken down into separate steps:

1. The *hypothalamus* brain area perceives a threatening stressor and sends a signal to the *adrenal glands*.

2. The *adrenal medulla* within the adrenal glands triggers the release of the hormone *adrenaline* into the endocrine system and the neurotransmitter *noradrenaline* in the brain.

3. Physical changes are incurred within the body that help an individual to fight or run away from the threatening stressor, for example, an attacker:
   - *Increased heart rate* – speeds up blood flow to vital organs and flow of adrenaline around the body
   - *Faster breathing rate* – increases oxygen intake
   - *Muscle tension* – improves reaction time and speed
   - *Pupil dilation* – improves vision
   - *Sweat production* – helps temperature control
   - *Reduced digestion and immune system functioning* – targets energy towards prioritised functioning, such as fighting and running

Practical application
Oxytocin sprays have been used to treat autism, as oxytocin seems to stimulate areas of the brain associated with social interaction, something that autistic people often have difficulties with. The sprays are used to facilitate the effectiveness of therapies.

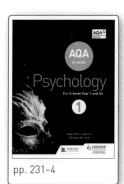

pp. 231–4

6 Psychopathology

Definitions of abnormality: deviation from social norms

Description

The *deviation from social norms* definition of abnormality implies that there is a 'correct' and an 'incorrect' way of behaving and that any deviation from the 'correct' way is abnormal. The social norms, to which there is an expectation for individuals to adhere, are therefore a set of unwritten rules of what is acceptable behaviour, which have been constructed by society. There is an argument that these norms are set by the ruling elite within a society and are more a means of policing people and maintaining social order than an objective definition of what is normal and abnormal. The deviation from social norms definition permits a distinction between what is seen as desirable and undesirable behaviour, classifying those exhibiting undesirable behaviour as *socially deviant*. This gives society, through its controlling institutions, like the health service, the right to intervene in people's lives in order to protect the rest of society and to 'treat' social deviants so that they can become 'normal' again and be returned to mainstream society. The definition can be seen as beneficial to abnormal individuals because deviants, such as those classed as sexually deviant, may be unable to recognise that their behaviour is maladaptive and therefore be unable to seek help by themselves. The deviation from social norms definition can also be seen to add a social dimension to the concept of abnormality, as it perceives the main purpose of mental health care as being to exclude from society individuals who are seen as behaving in unacceptable ways.

There are several types of social norms to which adherence is expected:

- *Situational/contextual norms,* where certain behaviours are expected/ not expected in certain situations. For example, it is acceptable for females to wear a bikini on the beach but not in the supermarket.
- *Developmental/age norms,* where certain behaviours are expected at different times in one's lifespan. For example, temper tantrums are perfectly acceptable for a 2-year-old to exhibit but not for a 40-year-old.
- *Cultural norms,* where certain behaviours are acceptable/unacceptable in different cultural settings, like homosexuality being accepted in Western cultures, but not in African ones.

✅ Strengths

✔ The social norms definition gives a clear indication of what is and what is not perceived as normal and this allows the relevant agencies, such as mental health practitioners, to know when they have a responsibility to intervene in people's lives. This is beneficial because it means individuals will get the clinical help that they probably would not have sought themselves if left to their own devices.

✔ The definition can be seen to establish norms of normality that apply in different circumstances, therefore giving a degree of flexibility that no other definition has. *Situational norms*, where the definition considers the social dimensions of behaviour, are where a behaviour seen as abnormal in one setting may be regarded as normal in another. For example, being naked in town is seen as abnormal, but not in a nudist colony. *Developmental norms* establish what behaviours are normal/abnormal at different ages. Playing hopscotch as a child is seen as normal, but not in adulthood. There are also *cultural norms* and *gender norms*, where normality changes across cultures and between genders, again showing the flexibility the definition offers.

❌ Limitations

✘ Szasz (1960) argued that the definition is used to justify discriminating against sections of society as a form of social control. Some countries, such as China, categorise political opponents as being abnormal and then forcibly treat them in mental institutions.

✘ There are individuals who adhere so strictly to social norms that they can be considered *conforming neurotics*. Such individuals fear rejection and ridicule so much that they conform rigidly to society's norms and worry excessively about them. This is a form of abnormality, yet the individuals are not classified as abnormal by the deviation from social norms definition.

✘ Social norms are not real in an objective sense, but are subjective, as they are based on the opinions of a society's elite and are then used to police those seen as challenging social order. Also, social norms refer to moral standards that change over time, like homosexuality once being classed as a mental disorder. A truly objective definition would not have such variations. Additionally, those who deviate from social norms may simply be individualistic or eccentric, rather than abnormal.

Practical application

For positive social change to occur, it is often necessary for social norms to be broken. This is a form of minority influence, where a minority slowly wins a majority over by going against mainstream social norms and changing people's belief systems. This is to be encouraged in organisations that require the formation of innovative ideas and practices.

pp. 147–8

6 Psychopathology

Definitions of abnormality: failure to function adequately

Description

The failure to function adequately definition of abnormality sees mental disorders as resulting from an inability to cope with day-to-day living. Behaviour is perceived as abnormal when individuals become so distressed with the pressures of everyday life that their behaviour becomes dysfunctional, for example, when an individual's ability to work properly is affected or when individuals cannot conduct normal interpersonal relationships. Due to an inability to cope with life, harmful behaviours are indulged in, like heavy drinking or drug taking. Such behaviours are themselves dysfunctional, but also contribute to further declines in personal functioning, leading to a diagnosis of abnormality.

Rosenhan & Seligman (1989) proposed that personal dysfunction has 7 features and that the more of these features an individual has, the more they are classed as abnormal:

1   *Personal distress*, which is seen as a key feature of abnormality and involves such things as depression and anxiety disorders

2   *Maladaptive behaviour*, which consists of exhibiting behaviour that prevents people from realising their life goals, both socially and at work

3   *Unpredictability*, which consists of exhibiting unexpected behaviours characterised by a loss of control, like mutilating oneself after a relationship is terminated

4   *Irrationality*, which consists of exhibiting behaviours non-explicable in any rational way, like heavy drinking in response to work pressures

5   *Observer discomfort*, which entails the exhibition of behaviours that cause discomfort to others, like behaving in an aggressive manner

6   *Violation of moral standards*, which consists of exhibiting behaviours that go against society's ethical standards, like being naked in a public place

7   *Unconventionality*, which entails the exhibition of non-standard behaviours, like dressing in the clothes of the opposite gender

An overall assessment of how well individuals can cope with life is made by clinicians using the *Global Assessment of Functioning scale* (GAF), which rates levels of social, occupational and psychological functioning. In general, this is a definition used by clinicians that focuses on individuals' perceptions of their own mental health and is judged through criteria such as 'can hold down a job', 'is able to dress themself' etc.

✔ Most people who seek clinical help do so because they see themselves as suffering from psychological problems that interfere with their ability to function normally, both socially and at work. Therefore, sufferers' perceptions of their problems match the criteria of the definition, giving it support.

✔ The GAF scale, used by clinicians to calculate an individual's overall level of functioning, is scored on a continuous scale. It therefore allows clinicians to see the degree to which individuals are abnormal and helps them to decide who needs what degree of psychiatric help.

✔ The definition permits judgement by knowledgeable others, as to whether individuals are functioning properly, because it focuses on observable and therefore measurable behaviour. This also allows the formation of a practical 'checklist' of factors that individuals can use to assess their own level of abnormality.

✔ As the definition recognises the importance of the role of the personal experience of individuals, it permits mental disorders to be regarded from the personal perspective of the individuals suffering from the disorders, therefore giving a greater depth of understanding to the definition.

✖ **Limitations**

✖ Although an individual's behaviour may be distressing to others and perceived as an inability to function adequately, it may bring no distress to the individual and be perceived by them as perfectly functional. For example, Stephen Gough is known as the 'naked rambler' for his long-distance walks that he conducts in the nude. He has been jailed many times for his behaviour, which he sees as perfectly normal and which causes him no distress.

✖ Mental disorders are not always accompanied by personal dysfunction; indeed the opposite may be true. Harold Shipman, a Lancashire doctor, displayed an outwardly normal disposition, while over a 23-year period as a doctor he murdered at least 215 of his patients before killing himself in prison.

✖ Some of the features comprising 'adequate functioning' are subjective and difficult to define and measure objectively. This also applies to individual differences between people; what is normal behaviour for introverts, like wearing non-flamboyant clothes, would be completely different for extroverts. The definition fails to incorporate this.

Fig 6.1 Harold Shipman

Practical application
A great practical application of the definition is that it permits a large element of self-diagnosis by individuals. Using a checklist of factors to assess their own level of abnormality, individuals are then able to seek clinical help through self-recognition that this is necessary. Most people receiving clinical help sought it themselves in the first instance.

pp. 148–9

6 Psychopathology

Definitions of abnormality: deviation from ideal mental health

Description

The deviation from ideal mental health definition of abnormality concentrates on identifying the characteristics and abilities people should possess in order to be considered normal. A lack of or impoverishment of these characteristics and abilities constitutes a diagnosis of abnormality. The definition therefore has a perception of mental disorder as being similar to that of physical health, in that an absence of wellbeing means that an individual is ill. Jahoda (1958) devised the concept of ideal mental health and identified set characteristics that individuals need to exhibit to be seen as normal. The more of these criteria an individual fails to realise, and the further away they are from meeting individual criteria, then the more abnormal they are considered to be. Similar to the deviation from social norms definition and the failure to function adequately definition, the deviation from ideal mental health definition also concentrates on behaviours and characteristics that are seen as desirable, rather than undesirable.

There are 6 characteristics of ideal mental health:

1. *Positive attitude towards oneself*, which involves having self-respect and a positive self-concept where individuals regard themselves favourably

2. *Self-actualisation*, where individuals should experience personal growth and development. Self-actualisation involves 'becoming everything one is capable of becoming'.

3. *Autonomy*, which concerns individuals being independent, self-reliant and able to make personal decisions

4. *Resistance to stress*, where individuals should be in possession of effective coping strategies in response to stress and should be able to cope with everyday anxiety-provoking situations

5. *Accurate perception of reality*, where individuals should be able to perceive the world in a non-distorted manner and possess an objective and realistic perception of the world

6. *Environmental mastery*, which concerns individuals being skilled in all aspects of their lives, both socially and occupationally and being able to meet the requirements of all situations they experience. Additionally, individuals should possess the flexibility to be able to adapt to changing life circumstances, both socially and occupationally.

✔ Strengths

- ✔ As the definition gives identification to specific types of dysfunction, it permits targeting of exact areas for mental health practitioners to work on when treating a person's abnormal condition. This can prove beneficial when treating different types of disorders – for example, focusing on the specific problem areas of a person with depression.

- ✔ A positive aspect to this definition is that it stresses positive accomplishments, rather than failures and distress, and therefore promotes a positive approach to mental disorders by focusing on what qualities are appropriate, rather than which ones are inappropriate.

- ✔ The definition can be seen to take a *holistic* approach, one that is interested in developing the whole person, rather than a *reductionist* approach that just focuses on individual areas of a person's behaviour.

- ✔ A positive aspect of the definition is that, as it identifies areas where personal weaknesses exist, it can be seen to be promoting self-growth by giving opportunities to improve on these areas.

❌ Limitations

❌ According to these criteria, most – if not all – people would be abnormal most of the time. Therefore, the criteria are over-demanding. For example, few people experience continual personal growth, indeed the opposite may be periodically common. Self-actualisation is seen as something that very few people achieve, so does this mean the majority of us are abnormal? The criteria may actually be *ideals* of mental health: how we would like to be, rather than how we actually are.

❌ The characteristics used to assess mental health are *culturally relative* and should not be used to judge people from other cultures and sub-cultures. For instance, some mental disorders only exist in certain cultures, such as *Koro*, found only in south-east Asia, China and Africa, which is a disorder concerning the belief that a man's penis is fatally retracting into his body. Therefore, Western cultural views of abnormality, like the deviation from ideal mental health definition, are not culture-free.

❌ Many of the criteria are subjective, being vague in description and rather hard to measure in any objective way. Measuring physical indicators of health is generally easy, for example by using blood tests and scans, but diagnosis of mental health is much trickier and relies largely upon the self-reports of patients who may not be reliable if they have a mental disorder.

Practical application
A practical application of the definition is that it permits identification of what is needed specifically to achieve normality. This therefore allows mental health practitioners to create personal targets for patients to work towards so that they can achieve better mental health.

Fig 6.2 The deviation from ideal mental health definition may be more about the ideal self than the actual self

pp. 150–1

6 Psychopathology
Definitions of abnormality: statistical infrequency

Description

The statistical infrequency definition of abnormality sees behaviours that are statistically rare as being abnormal. Data are collected about various behaviours and personal characteristics, so that their distributions throughout the general population can be calculated and plotted. This then allows the formation of *normal distributions* for these behaviours and characteristics. Normal distribution concerns the idea that for any given behaviour or characteristic there will be a spread of scores that forms a bell-shaped curve. Most people's scores occur on or around the mean and a decreasing amount of scores occur on either side of the mean, further away from the norm. This means there will be a symmetrical distribution of scores (as many scores below the mean as above the mean). Any scores that fall outside of normal distribution, which is usually seen as being 2 standard deviation points away from the mean (about 5 per cent of a population, which is 1 in 20 people), are regarded as abnormal in this definition. So taking intelligence, for example, data are collected on an individual's IQ scores (seen as being a valid measurement of intelligence, though this is disputed by many psychologists) and then used to plot the distribution of IQ scores on and around the mean. The mean score for IQ is supposed to be 100 IQ points and most individuals will be seen to score on or around this amount of measured intelligence. Decreasing amounts of people will have IQ scores that are further away from the norm (either above or below it) and therefore the data form the classic bell-shaped (also known as the Gaussian) curve. Two standard deviation points below the norm brings us to a score of 70 IQ points and 2 standard deviation points above the norm brings us to 130 IQ points. In terms of the definition, the 5 per cent of people in total who score below and above these levels are classed as abnormal, as they fall outside the normal distribution.

The statistical infrequency definition does nothing more than create the statistical criteria upon which behaviours and personal characteristics can be deemed to be normal or abnormal; it makes no judgements about quality of life or the nature of mental disorders.

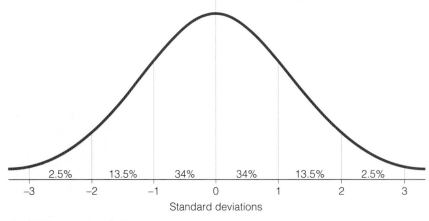

Fig 6.3 Standard deviation

✔ The definition makes no value judgements about what is or is not abnormal. So, for example, homosexuality, once defined as a mental disorder under earlier versions of diagnostic criteria, would not be seen under this definition as 'morally wrong' or 'unacceptable' – instead it would be viewed merely as less statistically frequent than heterosexuality.

✔ There are definite examples of situations where statistically determined criteria can be used to decide abnormality – for example, with mental retardation, where individuals will suffer with severe learning difficulties and thus need assistance with day-to-day living.

✔ The definition is a very objective one, as it relies on real, unbiased data. Once data about a behaviour or personal characteristic have been collected, the information becomes a very non-subjective and value-free means of deciding who is abnormal and who is not.

✔ The definition also permits an overall view of which particular behaviours and characteristics are infrequent within the population and so can help us determine which behaviours and characteristics can be regarded as abnormal.

✗ A major weakness of the definition is that not all statistically infrequent behaviours are actually abnormal. Many statistically rare behaviours and characteristics are desirable rather than undesirable ones. For example, being highly intelligent (determined by normal distribution, as being above around 130 IQ points) is indeed statistically rare, but would be regarded as desirable.

✗ Although the definition claims to be objective in not using value judgements, but instead statistical data, to determine what deviations in behaviour and characteristics are to be considered abnormal, a judgement is made about where exactly to draw the line. Indeed some mental disorders, like depression, vary greatly between individuals in terms of severity, but the definition does not account for this.

✗ Not all abnormal behaviours are statistically infrequent. Some statistically frequent and therefore 'normal' behaviours are actually abnormal. For instance, about 10 per cent of people are chronically depressed at some point in their lives, which would be so common as not to be seen as statistically rare and hence abnormal.

Practical application

A practical application of the definition is that as it is based purely on objective data, with no subjective judgements made about what is and what is not abnormal, it gives mental health practitioners a clear indication of when an individual needs clinical help. It can therefore be used as objective evidence to decide when an individual needs treatment.

pp. 151–3

6 Psychopathology
Characteristics of phobias, depression and OCD

Phobias

Everyone experiences anxiety – it is a natural response to potentially dangerous stimuli. Phobias, however, are anxiety disorders characterised by extreme irrational fears that go beyond any real risk. These can be very enduring, lasting for many years. Around 10 per cent of people will suffer from a phobia at some point in their lives, with females having twice the incidence of phobias as males. Most phobias emerge in childhood, but lessen in strength during adulthood. Sufferers generally have insight into their phobias and know that their fears and reactions are irrational, but they cannot consciously control them. Phobias divide into:

- *simple phobias*, involving fears of specific things, like coulrophobia (fear of clowns). Simple phobias further divide into sub-types of *animal phobias*, *injury phobias*, *situational phobias* and *natural environment phobias*.
- *social phobias*, involving being over-anxious in social situations, like giving public speeches
- *agoraphobia*, involving fear of leaving home or a safe place.

Characteristics of phobias

Behavioural

- *Avoidance responses* – efforts are made to avoid anxiety-producing situations.
- *Disruption of functioning* – severe disability to everyday working and social functioning occurs.

Emotional

- *Persistent, excessive fear* – high levels of anxiety are produced by phobic stimuli.
- Fear from exposure to phobic stimulus – production of immediate fear response to phobic stimulus.

Cognitive

- *Recognition of exaggerated anxiety* – phobics are consciously aware that their anxiety levels are over-stated.

Fig 6.4 Coulrophobia is a fear of clowns

Depression

About 20 per cent of people will suffer from depression, with women twice as vulnerable as men, especially in adolescence, a time where many people experience body dissatisfaction and low self-esteem. Depression is a mood disorder characterised by feelings of despondency and hopelessness, generally occurring in cycles. The average age of onset is in ones 20s and 10 per cent of people with severe depression commit suicide. There are 2 main types: *unipolar depression*, which is where a constant low mood is experienced, and *bipolar depression*, where sufferers swing between elevated (high) and despondent (low) moods. Depression is also broken down into *endogenous depression*, which is related to internal biochemical factors, and *exogenous depression*, which is related to stressful experiences. At least 5 *symptoms* (clinical characteristics) must be apparent every day for 2 weeks for depression to be diagnosed.

Characteristics of depression

Behavioural

- *Loss of energy* – sufferers experience reduced energy levels.
- *Social impairment* – reduced levels of interaction with friends and family occur.

Emotional

- *Loss of enthusiasm* – sufferers experience a lessened interest in, and pleasure of, everyday activities.

- *Sense of worthlessness* – persistent feelings of reduced worth and inappropriate sensations of guilt are experienced.

Cognitive

- *Reduced concentration* – difficulties with paying and maintaining attention, as well as slowed-down thinking and indecisiveness, can be experienced.
- *Poor memory* – difficulties with retrieval of memories can occur.

OCD

About 2 per cent of people have obsessive–compulsive disorder (OCD), an anxiety disorder characterised by persistent, recurrent, unpleasant thoughts and repetitive, ritualistic behaviours. Obsessions are the things that sufferers think about, while compulsions are the behaviours they indulge in as a result of the obsessions. Obsessions generally comprise forbidden or inappropriate ideas and visual images that are not based in reality, like being convinced that germs lurk everywhere, and these lead to feelings of extreme anxiety. Common obsessions include contamination, fear of losing control, perfectionism, sex and religion. Female obsessions tend to be more about contamination, while male ones can concern sex and religion more. Compulsions consist of intense, uncontrollable urges to perform repetitive tasks in order to reduce the anxiety caused by obsessive ideas, such as constantly washing yourself to get rid of the germs. There is a realisation that the obsessions and compulsions are inappropriate, but they cannot be consciously controlled. OCD symptoms often overlap with those of autism and Tourette's syndrome.

Characteristics of OCD

Behavioural

- *Hinders everyday functioning* – obsessive ideas create such high levels of anxiety that the ability to perform everyday actions is severely hindered.
- *Social impairment* – anxiety levels are so high that they limit the ability to conduct meaningful interpersonal relationships.

Emotional

- *Extreme anxiety* – persistent inappropriate ideas and visual images create excessive levels of anxiety.

Cognitive

- *Attentional bias* – perception tends to focus primarily on anxiety-generating stimuli.
- *Recurrent and persistent thoughts* – constantly repeated, obsessive, intrusive thoughts and ideas are experienced.

Practical application

Characteristics of mental disorders like phobias, depression and OCD allow clinicians to create 'checklists' that permit them to diagnose which particular disorder an individual may be suffering from. Such characteristics are written up into diagnostic criteria, such as the International Classification of Diseases (ICD) and the Diagnostic and Statistical Manual of Mental Disorders (DSM).

pp. 154–61

6 Psychopathology
The behavioural approach to explaining and treating phobias

Focal study

Brosnan & Thorpe (2006) investigated whether a fear of computers could be treated with SD. In Study 1, computer-anxious participants were given a 10-week programme of SD; while in Study 2, one group of computer-anxious participants were given a similar programme of SD and another group of computer-anxious participants received no treatment. In both studies there was also a control group of non-computer-anxious participants. In Study 1, anxiety levels in the computer-anxious participants declined to levels similar to the control group, while coping strategies noticeably improved. In Study 2, reduction in anxiety in the computer-anxious participants was 3 times greater than in the non-treated group over the course of a year. At the end of 1 year the computer-anxious participants' anxiety levels matched those of the control group, while the non-treated group remained significantly more anxious. This suggests that SD is effective in reducing technophobia (fear of technology).

OTHER STUDIES

- Watson & Rayner (1920) got a boy to hold a rat that he was not afraid of, while simultaneously scaring him by banging a bar behind his head. This was repeated over a period until the boy, when presented with the rat, would show fear. This illustrates how phobias can be learned through classical conditioning.

- Di Gallo (1996) showed that phobias of cars, developed through traumatic car accidents, were maintained by sufferers making avoidance responses, such as remaining at home rather than making car journeys to see friends. This illustrates how phobias are maintained by negative reinforcements associated with operant conditioning.

- King et al. (1998) reported that case studies showed that children acquired strong phobias through traumatic experiences, demonstrating the role of classical conditioning in the development of phobias, where a fear response becomes associated with an originally neutral stimulus.

Description

The behavioural explanation sees phobias as learned through experience via the process of association. The *two-process model* sees phobias as being learned through *classical conditioning*, with the maintenance of phobias occurring through *operant conditioning*.

- Classical conditioning sees a neutral stimulus becoming associated with a fear response so that the neutral stimulus produces the fear response on its own. For example, if a person gets mugged at night, then the neutral stimulus of night-time could become paired with a fear response, so that a person develops a phobia of the dark.

- With operant conditioning, a behaviour that is rewarding *reinforces*

Fig 6.5 Systematic desensitisation involves a step-by-step approach to a feared object or situation

✔ Acquisition of phobias can also be explained by *social learning theory* (SLT), where phobias are learned through observation and imitation. As SLT is another type of learning based on behaviourism, it gives added support to the explanation.

✔ The success of behavioural treatments like SD in treating phobias suggests that behavioural explanations of the acquisition and maintenance of phobias are valid.

✔ Behavioural explanations can be combined with biological ones to give a better understanding of phobias. The idea of *genetic vulnerability* explains how some individuals inherit an increased susceptibility to developing phobias, which then occur if certain environmental experiences occur for an individual.

the behaviour (makes it likely to occur again). So when an *avoidance response* is made to reduce the chances of contact with a phobic stimulus, it is *negatively reinforcing* – it reduces the fear response and thus the phobia is maintained, as the sufferer repeatedly makes reinforcing avoidance responses.

Systematic desensitisation (SD) is a behavioural therapy for treating phobias and involves a sufferer learning relaxation techniques, which are then used to repeatedly reduce anxiety, as the sufferer goes through a progressive hierarchy of exposure to the phobic stimulus – for example, a step-by-step approach to holding a spider to reduce a fear of the beasties.

✘ There are other valid, non-behavioural explanations of phobias, such as cognitive explanations that focus on faulty thought processes occurring between stimuli and responses and the evolutionary explanation, which sees phobias as having become widespread through the process of natural selection due to their adaptive survival value.

✘ SD is only really suitable for patients who are able to learn and use relaxation strategies, which is not always an easy thing for those experiencing high levels of anxiety. They also need to have imaginations vivid enough to conjure up images of phobic stimuli.

✘ The behavioural explanation is weakened by the fact that not everyone experiencing traumatic events, like a car crash, goes on to develop a phobia associated with the event.

Practical application
As well as SD, there are other useful behavioural treatments of phobias, like *flooding*, which involves direct confrontation with a feared stimulus. There are even smartphone apps based on SD which have been used to successfully treat phobias.

pp. 163–71

6 Psychopathology
The cognitive approach to explaining and treating depression

Focal study

Beevers *et al.* (2010) investigated whether brain areas associated with cognitive control were affected by emotional stimuli in participants with depression. Thirteen females with low levels of depression were compared with 14 females with high levels of depression. Participants were given 3 facial stimuli cues: happy, sad and neutral (as well as a control geometric-shape cue). A single cue was presented on a screen along with 1 of 2 target stimuli (either * or **). Time taken to recognise which target stimulus was presented was measured. Participants simultaneously had their brains scanned. Lower levels of activation were found in the high depression group in brain areas requiring cognitive control over emotional stimuli (when processing happy and sad faces) but no differences were found between the two groups in brain areas not requiring such cognitive control (neutral faces and geometric shapes). This supports the cognitive explanation that people with higher levels of depression have problems activating brain areas associated with cognitive control of emotional information.

Description

The *cognitive approach* sees depression as occurring as a result of maladaptive (irrational) thought processes. Beck (1987) saw people becoming depressed through *negative schemas* (tendencies to perceive the world negatively), consisting of:

- *ineptness schemas* that make people with depression expect to fail
- *self-blame schemas* that make people with depression feel responsible for all misfortunes
- *negative self-evaluation schemas* that constantly remind people with depression of their worthlessness

and fuelled by *cognitive biases* (tendencies to think in particular ways) that make individuals misperceive reality in a negative way.

OTHER STUDIES

- Boury *et al.* (2001) used the Beck depression inventory to monitor participants' negative thoughts and found that people with depression misinterpret facts and experiences in a negative way and feel hopeless about the future. This supports Beck's cognitive theory.

- Koster *et al.* (2005) showed participants a screen with positive, negative or neutral words on it. Then a square appeared on the screen and participants were asked to press a button to show where it was. He found that depressed participants took longer to disengage from depressive words than non-depressed participants. This supports the cognitive theory that depressives over-focus on negative stimuli.

- McIntosh & Fischer (2000) investigated whether the negative triad contains the proposed 3 distinct types of negative thought. They found no separation of negative thought, but instead a 1-dimensional negative perception of self. This suggests that a negative triad of separate types of negative thought does not exist.

Fig 6.6 Beck's negative triad

- ✔ The explanation is supported by the existence of a wealth of research evidence supporting the idea of cognitive vulnerability being linked to the onset of depression, with people with depression tending to selectively attend to negative stimuli.

- ✔ Cognitive therapies for depression have proven to be very effective compared to therapies based on other explanations, which suggests the explanation may have a higher validity than other explanations.

- ✔ The explanation acknowledges that non-cognitive aspects, like genes, development and early experiences, can lead to negative thinking patterns, which then leads to the onset of depression. This gives the theory greater explanatory power.

Negative schemas and cognitive biases maintain the *negative triad*, three pessimistic thought patterns concerning the *self*, the *world* and the *future*.

Ellis' *ABC model* sees depression occurring through an *activating agent* (where an event occurs), a *belief* held about the event and a *consequence* involving a response to the event. Cognitive treatments are based on modifying maladaptive thought processes to alter behavioural and emotional states – for example, *rational emotive behaviour therapy* (REBT), which seeks to make irrational and negative thinking more rational and positive. Therapists help patients realise how irrational their thinking is and encourage them to practise more optimistic thinking by *reframing*, which involves reinterpretation of the ABC in a more positive and logical way.

❌ **Negative evaluation**

- ✘ The cognitive approach has difficulties in explaining and treating the manic component of bipolar depression, lessening support for the theory as an overall explanation for depression.

- ✘ Most of the evidence concerning negative thought patterns and depression is correlational and does not therefore show that negative thinking causes depression. Beck believed it was a bi-directional relationship where depressed thoughts cause depression and vice versa.

- ✘ The treatment aetiology fallacy argues that the fact that cognitive therapies are effective in treating depression does not necessarily give support to the cognitive explanation on which they are based.

Practical application

Another effective cognitive therapy for treating depression is the treatment of negative automatic thoughts (TNAT), which, like REBT, works by restructuring maladaptive ways of thinking into more adaptive, rational ways of thinking.

pp. 172–83

6 Psychopathology
The biological approach to explaining and treating OCD

Focal study

Koran *et al.* (2000) investigated whether treating non-responsive forms of OCD with simultaneous drug treatments was more effective than single-drug treatments. Ten patients who had not responded to 10 weeks of treatment with the SRI antidepressant fluoxetine were the participants. All participants had been diagnosed with OCD for at least a year. Treatment with fluoxetine continued but increasing levels of another atypical antipsychotic drug, olanzapine, were also given for an additional period of 8 weeks. Nine participants completed the treatment and it was found that mean OCD symptom scores dropped by 16 per cent, with 1 patient showing a 68 per cent improvement and 2 others 30 and 29 per cent improvements. This suggests that giving simultaneous drug therapies can be more effective than single-drug treatment with resistant forms of OCD. However, 6 participants did experience significant weight increase, illustrating the possible side effects of such treatments.

OTHER STUDIES

- Hu (2006) compared serotonin activity levels between sufferers and non-sufferers of OCD and found that serotonin levels were significantly lower in OCD sufferers. This gives support to the idea that the neurotransmitter is involved in the development of the disorder.

- Fallon & Nields (1994) reported that 40 per cent of people contracting Lyme's disease incur neural damage resulting in psychiatric conditions like OCD, supporting the idea that OCD may develop from damage to brain mechanisms.

- Stewart *et al.* (2007) used gene mapping on sufferers and non-sufferers of OCD, to find a link to chromosome 14 marker D14S588, indicating a possible genetic link to the condition.

- Julien (2007) reviewed studies of the effectiveness of SSRI antidepressants in treating OCD and reported that although symptoms do not fully disappear, between 50 and 80 per cent of patients show improvements that allow them to live a fairly normal lifestyle. This supports the effectiveness of the treatment.

Description

The biological approach sees obsessive–compulsive disorder (OCD) as occurring by physiological means through genetic transmission and faulty brain mechanisms.

The genetic explanation focuses on the degree to which OCD is inherited. Findings from twin and gene mapping studies indicate a genetic link, with particular genes seen as increasing vulnerability to the disorder. There is a possibility of varying rates of genetic influence upon different sub-types of OCD.

Some forms of OCD are linked to breakdowns in immune system functioning, like streptococcal throat infections, Lyme's disease and influenza. This indicates that OCD may also develop

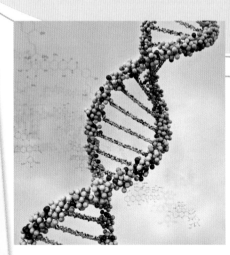

Fig 6.7 Gene mapping studies allow researchers to test the genetic explanation

from damage to brain mechanisms, with children more at risk from such factors than adults. PET scans have shown relatively low levels of serotonin activity in the brains of OCD sufferers. As drugs that increase serotonin activity reduce the symptoms of OCD, this suggests that the neurotransmitter may play a key role in determining the condition. Research also indicates faulty functioning of the orbital frontal cortex brain area, which results in sufferers having difficulties in ignoring impulses, so they turn into obsessions, resulting in compulsive behaviour.

The main biological treatment is drugs, with antidepressants that heighten serotonin activity most favoured.

Practical application

Aside from drug therapies, another biological treatment of OCD is that of psychosurgery, but only for severe cases of the disorder which are non-responsive to other treatments. A more recent and less invasive treatment is deep-brain stimulation, which uses magnetic pulses to block out obsessional thoughts.

pp. 184–94

7 Research methods
Experimental method and design

Description

With the experimental method, researchers manipulate an *independent variable* (IV) between experimental conditions to see its effect on a *dependent variable* (DV), which is always a measurement of some kind. Participants should be randomly allocated (selected without bias) to the experimental conditions. *Controls* prevent *extraneous variables* (variables other than the IV that could affect the value of the DV) from becoming *confounding variables* that 'confuse' the results. *Standardisation* involves each participant performing an experiment under the same conditions to reduce the chances of confounding variables. *Causality* (cause and effect relationships) is thus established. For instance, caffeine consumption (IV) could be manipulated to assess the effect on reaction times (DV), with all other variables, like amount of sleep, food consumed etc., kept constant between participants.

Types of experiments

- *Laboratory experiments* are performed in a controlled environment, permitting the control of most variables, with participants randomly allocated to testing groups.
- *Field experiments* are performed in the 'real world' rather than a laboratory, with the IV manipulated by researchers and other variables controlled.
- *Natural experiments* occur where the independent variable varies naturally, with the researcher recording the effect on the DV. Participants are not randomly allocated.
- *Quasi experiments* occur where the IV occurs naturally, like whether participants are male or female. Participants are not therefore randomly allocated. This method is often used when it is unethical to manipulate an IV.

✔ Strengths of experiments

Laboratory

- ✔ With extraneous variables being controlled, causality can be established, i.e. that changes in the value of the DV are due to manipulation of the IV.
- ✔ Other researchers can exactly replicate the study to check results.

Field, natural and quasi

- ✔ As they occur in real-world settings, findings have high ecological validity and therefore are generalisable to other settings.
- ✔ As participants are often unaware they are being studied, there are fewer demand characteristics and therefore participants behave naturally.

✘ Weaknesses of experiments

Laboratory

- ✘ High degrees of control are artificial, which means that results lack *ecological validity* and are not generalisable to real-life settings.
- ✘ *Demand characteristics* may occur, where participants attempt to guess the purpose of the study and respond accordingly.

Field, natural and quasi

- ✘ As it is more difficult to control extraneous variables, causality is harder to establish.
- ✘ It is difficult to replicate such experiments, as the lack of control means testing conditions are rarely the same again.

Experimental conditions have different forms of the IV, with the *control condition* acting as a comparison against the *experimental condition*. Three types of design exist, each with strengths and weaknesses.

- *Repeated measures design* (RMD) – the same participants perform each condition, therefore participants are tested against themselves under different forms of the IV.
- *Matched participants design* (MPD) – a special kind of RMD with participants pre-tested and matched on important variables into similar pairs. One of each pair is randomly allocated into the experimental condition and one into the control condition.
- *Independent groups design* (IGD) – different participants perform each testing condition, making them independent of each other, with participants randomly allocated to different conditions. Each participant therefore performs only one condition of an experiment.

✅ Strengths of experimental designs

RMD

✔ As each participant performs in all conditions, they are compared against themselves, so there are no *participant variables* (individual differences between participants) and differences in findings are due to manipulations of the IV.

✔ As participants perform in all conditions, fewer participants are needed.

IGD

✔ As different participants perform different conditions, there are no order effects.

✔ Demand characteristics are reduced, as participants only perform one condition each.

MPD

✔ As participants do all conditions, there are no order effects.

✔ As participants do all conditions, there is less chance of demand characteristics by 'guessing' the purpose of the study.

Weaknesses of experimental designs

RMD

✗ *Order effects* occur, where the order in which participants perform the experimental conditions affects results, e.g. through learning or fatigue. Order effects are *counterbalanced*, where half the participants do one condition first and half do the other condition first.

IGD

✗ As participants only perform one condition, more participants are required to produce the same amount of data than in a RMD.

✗ There is a risk of *participant variables*, as findings may be due to participants' individual differences, rather than manipulations of the IV.

MPD

✗ As participants only perform in one condition, twice as many participants are required than with a RMD.

✗ MPD requires pre-testing and matching on important variables and therefore is time-consuming.

pp. 258–62

7 Research methods
Non-experimental methods and design
Description

Non-experimental (*alternative*) research methods differ from experiments in that they do not have an IV or a DV and are not conducted under controlled conditions. They are therefore difficult to replicate and do not show causality (cause and effect relationships). Each method has strengths and weaknesses and is more appropriate to different types of research aims.

Correlational analysis

Correlational analysis involves assessing the degree of relationship between 2 or more co-variables, for example between the number of hours' sleep and the score on a memory test. A *positive* correlation occurs when one co-variable increases as another co-variable increases, for example sales of umbrellas increase as the number of rainy days increases. A *negative* correlation occurs when one co-variable decreases while another increases, for example sales of bikinis decrease as the number of rainy days increases. *Zero correlations* occur when there is no association between co-variables. A *correlational co-efficient* is a numerical value expressing the degree to which co-variables are related. Measurements range between +1.0, a perfect positive correlation, and −1.0, a perfect negative correlation.

✔ Strengths

- ✔ Correlations do not require manipulation and are used when experiments would be unethical.
- ✔ Once correlations are established, predictions can be made, like how many umbrellas will be sold on rainy days.

✖ Weaknesses

- ✖ Correlations are not conducted under controlled conditions and therefore do not show causality.
- ✖ Apparently low correlations can actually be statistically significant if the number of scores used is sufficiently high.

OBSERVATIONS

Naturalistic observations involve measuring naturally occurring behaviour in real-world situations, like *Festinger's (1957) study* where he infiltrated a cult who were predicting the end of the world. *Controlled* observations are conducted under controlled laboratory conditions, like *Zimbardo's prison simulation* (see **page 8**). *Participant* observations involve researchers being actively involved in the behaviour being assessed. *Non-participant* observations involve researchers not being actively involved in the behaviour being assessed. *Overt* observations involve the participants knowing that they are being observed, while in *covert* observations participants do not know that they are being observed.

✔ Strengths

- ✔ Observations have high *external validity*, as they involve natural behaviour in a real-life setting and so can be generalised to other settings.
- ✔ As participants are usually unaware of being observed, there are few *demand characteristics*.

✖ Weaknesses

- ✖ It can be difficult to remain unobserved and make accurate, full observations.
- ✖ As observations are not conducted under controlled conditions, they are difficult to replicate to check the reliability and validity of findings.

SELF-REPORTS: QUESTIONNAIRES

Self-reports involve participants detailing information about themselves without researcher intervention.

Questionnaires are a self-report method where participants give answers to pre-set written questions usually involving opinions, attitudes, beliefs and behaviour. *Closed* questions involve limited responses set by researchers, such as 'yes/no' tick boxes. Answers are easy to quantify, but restricted. *Open* questions allow participants to answer fully in their own words and therefore give a greater depth and freedom of expression, but are less easy to quantify and analyse.

✓ Strengths

- ✓ Large samples can be generated by posting out questionnaires, which also means researchers do not have to be present when they are completed.
- ✓ Questionnaires obtain lots of data in a relatively quick time.

✗ Weaknesses

- ✗ There is a possibility of *idealised* and *socially desirable* answers, with participants answering in the way they think they should, rather than giving honest answers.
- ✗ Questionnaires, especially those with closed questions, are not suitable for sensitive issues requiring careful and detailed understanding.

SELF-REPORTS: INTERVIEWS

Interviews involve asking participants face-to-face questions. *Structured* interviews involve asking identical, simple, quantitative questions to all participants. *Unstructured* interviews involve an informal discussion on set topics and produce mainly qualitative data. *Semi-structured* interviews involve a mixture of structured and unstructured questions.

✓ Strengths

- ✓ Both quantitative and qualitative data are produced that offer a greater variety and depth of findings.
- ✓ With unstructured and semi-structured interviews, follow-up questions can be asked to explore interesting answers.

✗ Weaknesses

- ✗ Interviewers can bias responses through their appearance, age, gender etc.
- ✗ Some participants may not have the verbal skills to express themselves fully.

Fig 7.2 Observational studies usually involve observing behaviour in real-world settings, for example observations of football hooliganism

pp. 262–70

7 Research methods
Scientific processes

> ### Aims
>
> Aims are research objectives, exact statements of why studies are conducted, for instance to investigate whether differing amounts of sleep affect concentration levels. Aims should incorporate what is being studied and what the studies are trying to achieve.

Hypotheses

Hypotheses are more objectively precise than aims and are testable predictions of what is expected to happen. There are 2 types of hypothesis:

1   The *experimental* hypothesis predicts that differences in the DV will be outside the boundaries of chance (known as *significant differences*), as a result of manipulation of the IV. An example is 'that participants receiving 8 hours' sleep last night will perform significantly better on a test of concentration than those receiving 4 hours' sleep last night'. The term 'experimental hypothesis' is used with experiments; other research methods refer to 'alternative hypotheses'.

2   The *null* hypothesis predicts that the IV will not affect the DV and that any differences found will not be outside the boundaries of chance, i.e. will not be significantly different. An example is 'that participants receiving 8 hours' sleep last night will not perform significantly better on a test of concentration than those receiving 4 hours' sleep last night. Any differences found will be due to chance factors'. One of these two hypotheses will be supported by the findings and accepted, while the other will be rejected.

There are 2 types of experimental/alternative hypothesis:

1   *Directional* (*one-tailed*) hypotheses predict the direction that the results will lie in. An example is 'that participants running 400 metres on an athletics track while being watched by an audience of their peers will run significantly quicker times than those running without an audience'.

2   *Non-directional* (*two-tailed*) hypotheses predict a difference in the results, but not the direction the results will lie in. An example is 'that there will be a significant difference in times achieved between participants running 400 metres on an athletics track while being watched by an audience of their peers and those running without an audience'.

Directional hypotheses are used when previous research gives an indication of which way findings will lie.

> ### OPERATIONALISATION OF VARIABLES
>
> Operationalisation concerns objectively defining variables in an easily understandable manner, so that an *independent variable* (IV) can be manipulated (altered between testing conditions) and its effect on a *dependent variable* (DV) measured. For example, if researching the effect of sleep on concentration, the IV could be operationalised as the amount of sleep the previous night and the DV as the score on a test of concentration. Without accurate operationalisation, results may be unreliable and invalid; therefore it is crucial to operationalise IVs and DVs accurately. However, this can be difficult — for example how can 'anger' be accurately operationalised?

Investigator effects

Investigator effects are the ways in which researchers can unconsciously influence research. These may be:

- *major physical characteristics* like the age and gender of researchers
- *minor physical characteristics* like the accent and tone of voice of researchers
- *unconscious bias* in the interpretation of data.

The *double-blind technique* reduces investigator effects because neither participants nor researchers know which conditions participants are in.

PILOT STUDIES

Pilot studies are small-scale 'practice' investigations allowing procedural improvements and the removal of methodological errors. Participants can point out flaws, like the presence of demand characteristics. Pilot studies show what kind of results are expected and if there is any possibility of significant results. They permit the quality of research to be improved and help avoid unnecessary time and effort being wasted, for example, by performing lengthy studies only to find that, due to unexpected errors and problems, the results are invalid and the study will have to be altered and repeated.

Fig 7.3 The physical appearance of an investigator can unconsciously affect the behaviour of participants in studies

pp. 271, 276

83

7 Research methods

Observational design, questionnaire construction and interviews

Observational design

There are several ways to gather data from observations, including visual and audio recordings, and 'on-the-spot' note-taking, using rating scales and coding categories. Observational studies work best when time is taken to create effective behavioural categories.

Behavioural categories

Observers need to agree on a grid or coding sheet that truly represents the behaviour being observed. For instance, if observers wish to observe the effect of age and gender on the speed of car driving they might wish to create behavioural categories like 'Distracted', 'Talking', 'Using mobile phone' and 'Concentrating' (see Table 7.1) and then code an individual driver's behaviour using agreed ratings. Coding can involve numbers, like the apparent age of the driver, or letters to denote characteristics such as gender, e.g. 'M' for male, as well as observed behaviours, like using 'T' for a driver that was talking. Observed behaviours can also be rated on structured scales, from 1 to 5, for example, to indicate the degree of safe driving.

Table 7.1 Behavioural categories of driving behaviour

Driver	Sex (M/F)	Age (estimate)	Number of passengers	Observed behaviour	Type of car	Speed (estimate in km per hour)	Safe driving rating (1 = very safe; 5 = very unsafe)
A	M	55	0	M-P	Ford	40	2
B	F	21	2	T	VW	30	5
C	F	39	3	D	BMW	50	3
D etc.	M	70	0	C	Jensen	60	5

Observed behaviour code

D = Distracted   M-P = Using mobile phone
T = Talking   C = Concentrating

Sampling procedures

It is often difficult to observe all behaviour, especially continuous (non-stop) behaviour. Placing behaviour into categories helps, but there are also different types of sampling procedure (methods of recording data) that can be used. These involve selecting some of the behaviour to observe and record, with the aim being to select representative behaviour.

- One sampling procedure is *event sampling*, where the number of times a behaviour occurs in a target individual (or individuals) is recorded.
- Another sampling procedure is *time sampling*, where behaviour is recorded at set intervals, for instance what behaviour is seen every 30 seconds.

Inter-observer reliability

Inter-observer reliability occurs when independent observers code behaviour in the same way. This lessens the chance of *observer bias* where an observer sees what they want/expect to see. To establish inter-observer reliability, clearly described behavioural categories need to be created that do not overlap with each other. Video-taping observed behaviour means inter-observer reliability can be checked at a later date.

Questionnaires

A problem with questionnaires is their low response rate. Therefore, it is important to construct questionnaires in a way that maximises the chances of participants completing and returning them.

- *Aims* Having a precise aim not only allows participants to understand the purpose of the questionnaire, but also allows researchers to construct questions that fit the aim.
- *Length* Having unnecessary questions and over-long questions increases the chances that participants will not give the questions full consideration, or will not even complete the questionnaire.
- *Previous questionnaires* Questionnaires that have proved successful in gaining high return rates and generating useful answers should be used as a basis for the construction of a new questionnaire.
- *Question formation* To generate meaningful answers and to increase completion rates questions should be concise, unambiguous and easy to understand. It is also best if questions stick to single points to avoid becoming over-complex and confusing.
- *Pilot study* A questionnaire should be tested out on a small group of individuals who provide detailed and honest feedback on all aspects of the questionnaire's design. This means corrections/adjustments can be made before the questionnaire is used on the actual sample of participants.
- *Measurement scales* Questionnaires often use measurement scales involving a series of statements, with participants choosing a score that reflects the statement they opt for. However, if participants do not fully understand a question they will tend to choose the middle score, which can give a false impression of their actual attitude to that question. Therefore, when constructing such questions it is important that the question and the statements to choose from are easy to understand.

Rate your level of agreement with the following statement:
'Vigorous regular exercise is good for your health.'

1	2	3	4	5
Strongly agree	Agree	Undecided	Disagree	Strongly disagree

Effective questionnaires also use a mix of *closed* questions, which allow a limited range of responses (like yes/no answers) and generate *quantitative data* (occurring as numbers), and *open* questions, which allow participants to answer fully in their own words and generate *qualitative data* (non-numerical).

DESIGN OF INTERVIEWS

The effectiveness of interviews is dependent on the appropriateness of the interviewer. The choice of this person is affected by several factors:

- *Gender and age* – can particularly affect answers on questions of a sensitive sexual nature.
- *Ethnicity* – fuller more honest answers are gained with interviewers of the same ethnic background as the interviewee.
- *Personal characteristics* – appearance, accent, amount of formality etc. of an interviewer can all affect the answers gained. Effective interviewers adapt their style to suit different interviewees.

pp. 263–8

7 Research methods
Sampling techniques and ethics

Sampling techniques

A sample is a part of a population and should be as representative as possible. It should possess the same characteristics as the population from which it is drawn. Several sampling techniques exist.

Random sampling

Random sampling occurs where all members of a target population have an equal chance of being selected. Computer generated random number lists can be used.

 Strengths

✔ Selection is unbiased and the sample should be fairly representative.

❌ **Weaknesses**

✘ Sometimes random sampling is impractical, for example where not all members of a population are available.

✘ Samples can still be unrepresentative, for example where all females are selected.

Opportunity sampling

Opportunity sampling involves using whoever is available.

✔ **Strengths**

✔ Such samples are easy to obtain.

✔ It is the only sampling type available with natural experiments.

❌ **Weaknesses**

✘ It is often unrepresentative, for example where all students are selected.

✘ As participants can decline to take part it can turn into self-selected sampling.

Self-selected sampling

Self-selected sampling involves using volunteers, usually responding to advertisements.

✔ **Strengths**

✔ It involves minimal effort to obtain participants.

✔ There is less chance of the 'screw you phenomenon' (where participants deliberately sabotage the study).

❌ **Weaknesses**

✘ It often provides biased samples, as volunteers can be a certain 'type' of person and be so eager to please that demand characteristics occur.

Systematic sampling

Systematic sampling involves taking every nth person from a list of the target population. This includes calculating the size of the population and assessing how big the sample needs to be to work out what the sampling interval should be (how big n is).

✔ **Strengths**

✔ There is no bias in selection, so the sample should be fairly representative.

❌ **Weaknesses**

✘ Samples can still be unrepresentative if n coincides with a frequency trait, for example, if n = every fifth house in a street and every fifth house is flats occupied by young people.

Stratified sampling

Stratified sampling is a small-scale reproduction of a population and involves dividing a population into its *strata* (sub-parts) and then random sampling from each stratum. If one stratum has 15 per cent of the population, then 15 per cent of the sample is drawn from that stratum and so on.

 Strengths

✔ Sampling is unbiased, and as selection occurs from representative sub-groups, the sample should be fairly representative.

 Weaknesses

✘ It is time-consuming, and a detailed knowledge of strata is required.

Ethical issues

To protect the dignity and safety of participants, as well as the integrity of psychology, research should be conducted in an ethical manner. Full details of research should be submitted to the appropriate ethical committee for approval before commencing. The British Psychology Society (BPS) publishes a code of ethics that researchers should follow:

1 *Informed consent* – participants should be fully informed of the objectives and details of research to make a considered decision as whether to participate. Parental or guardian's consent is obtained for under 16s.

2 *Deception* – misleading of participants and withholding information should be avoided.

3 *Protection of participants* – participants should not be put at risk of harm and should leave a study in the same state they were in when they entered it.

4 *Right to withdraw* – participants should be aware that they can leave at any time; they should also be able to withdraw their data in the future.

5 *Confidentiality* – participants' data should not be disclosed to anyone, unless agreed in advance.

6 *Anonymity* – participants are referred to by numbers, not names, so that data cannot be traced back to them.

7 *Inducements to take part* – participants should not be encouraged to participate through offers of financial gain or other gratification.

8 *Observational research* – observations should only occur in environments where people would expect to be observed.

9 *Cost–benefit analysis* – only if the benefits of research, e.g. in terms of knowledge gained, outweigh the costs, e.g. in terms of possible harm to participants, should the research be undertaken.

If deception is unavoidable, there are measures that can be taken:

● *Presumptive consent* – people of a similar nature are given full details of a study and asked if they would have been willing to participate. If so, it is presumed the real participants would not object.

● *Prior general consent* – participants agree to be deceived, but without knowing how the deception will occur.

● *Debriefing* – immediately after a study finishes participants should be given full details and the right to withdraw their data. This applies to all studies, not just those involving deception, and also helps to alleviate possible psychological harm, so that participants leave in the same state they entered.

7 Research methods

Quantitative and qualitative data and introduction to statistical testing

(See also Presentation and display of quantitative data, **pages 90–91**)

Quantitative and qualitative data

Quantitative data are numerical (occur as numbers), and can be obtained, for example, by counting the number of times something happens. *Qualitative data* are non-numerical (occur in forms other than numbers), like someone describing their feelings. Quantitative data tend to be objective, reliable and simple, while qualitative data tend to be subjective, less reliable and more detailed. The 2 forms of data can be combined to give deeper understanding.

- Quantitative data are generally produced from experiments, observations, correlational studies and from structured interviews and closed questions in questionnaires. Qualitative data are generally produced from case studies and from unstructured interviews and open questions in questionnaires.
- Qualitative data give insight into feelings and thoughts, but analysis can be affected by researcher bias (the researcher's own interpretation of the data). However, qualitative data can be converted into quantitative data.

Primary and secondary data

- *Primary data* are original data collected specifically for a research aim and have not been published before.
- *Secondary data* are data originally collected for another research aim and have been published before.

Primary data are more reliable and valid than secondary data, as they have not been manipulated in any way. Secondary data drawn from several sources can help give a clearer insight into a research area than primary data can.

META-ANALYSIS

Meta-analysis is a process whereby a large number of studies, involving the same research aim and research methods, are reviewed together, with the combined data statistically tested to assess their overall effect. For instance, Smith & Bond (1993) did a meta-analysis of 133 conformity studies using the Asch paradigm to assess conformity levels in different cultures. As meta-analyses use data combined from many studies, they allow identification of trends and relationships that is not possible with individual studies. Meta-analyses are helpful when individual studies find contradictory or weak results, as they give a clearer overall picture.

Introduction to statistical testing

Research produces data which are analysed by statistical tests to see whether differences and relationships found between sets of data are significant or not. Three criteria need to be considered when choosing an appropriate statistical test:

- What design has been used – whether an *independent groups design* or a *repeated measures design* (including a matched pairs design) has been used
- What type of outcome is being tested for – is a difference or a relationship between 2 sets of data being sought?
- What level of measurement has been used – was the data produced of *nominal, ordinal* or *interval/ratio*

Levels of measurement

- *Nominal data* – consist of *frequencies*, for example, how many days of a week were rainy. Nominal data are relatively uninformative, for instance they would not tell us how rainy any particular day was.

- *Ordinal data* – involve putting data into *rank order*, for example finishing places of runners in a race. This is not fully informative, as although we know who are the better runners, we do not know by how much better they are.

- *Interval/ratio data* – involve data with standardised measuring distances, such as time. This is the most informative type of data. *Interval data* have an arbitrary zero point, for instance zero degrees temperature does not mean there is no temperature. *Ratio data* have an absolute zero point, for instance someone with zero pounds in their bank account has no money.

The sign test

An example of a statistical test is the *sign test* – used when a difference is predicted between 2 sets of data, data are of at least nominal level, and a repeated measures design (RMD)/matched pairs design (MPD) has been used. The sign test works by calculating the value of *s* (the less frequent sign) and comparing this value to those in a critical values table to see if the result is significant or not.

pp. 292–3, 299–302

7 Research methods

Presentation and display of quantitative data; distributions

Description

Quantitative data occur as numbers. They are often presented through graphs and tables, giving viewers an easily understandable visual interpretation of the findings from a study.

Graphs

Graphs should be fully and clearly labelled, on both the x-axis and the y-axis, and be appropriately titled. They are best presented if the y-axis (vertical) is three-quarters the length of the x-axis (horizontal). Only 1 graph should be used to display a set of data. Inappropriate scales should not be used, as these convey misleading, biased impressions. Different types of graphs exist for different forms of data.

Bar charts display data as separate, comparable categories, for example findings from young and old participants. The columns of the bars should be the same width and separated by spaces to show that the variable on the x-axis is not continuous. Data are 'discrete', occurring, for example, as the mean scores of several groups. Percentages, totals and ratios can also be displayed.

Histograms display continuous data, such as test scores, and these are displayed as they increase in value along the x-axis, without spaces between them to show their continuity. The frequency of the data is presented on the y-axis. The column width for each value on the x-axis is the same width per equal category interval so that the area of each column is proportional to the number of cases it represents on the histogram.

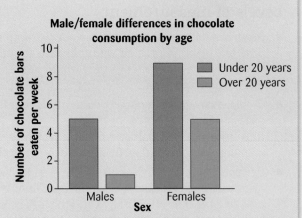

Fig 7.5 An example of a bar chart

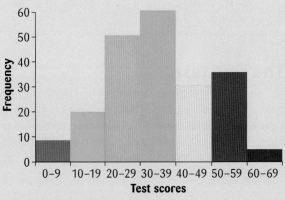

Fig 7.6 An example of a histogram

Frequency polygons (line graphs) are similar to histograms in that the data presented on the *x*-axis are continuous. A frequency polygon is constructed by drawing a line from the mid-point top of each column in a histogram to allow 2 or more frequency distributions to be displayed on the same graph, thus allowing them to be directly compared with each other.

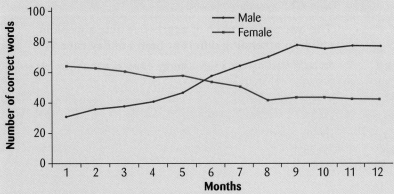

Fig 7.7 An example of a frequency polygon

Pie charts are used to show the frequency of categories of data as percentages. The pie is split into sections, each one representing the frequency of a category. Each section is colour coded, with an indication given as to what each section represents and its percentage score.

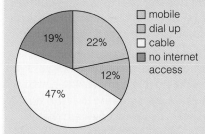

Fig 7.8 An example of a pie chart

Correlational data are plotted on *scattergrams*, which show the degree to which 2 co-variables are related.

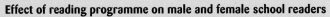

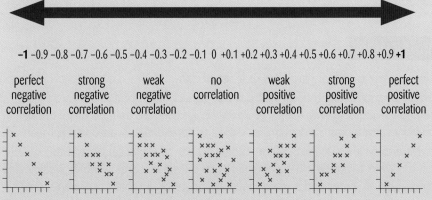

Fig 7.9 Scattergrams and strength of correlation

7 Research methods
Continued

TABLES

Tables do not present raw, unprocessed data such as individual scores. Rather they are used to present an appropriate summary of processed data, such as totals, means and ranges. The unprocessed data are given in the appendices of a study as a data table (i.e. a presentation of the raw scores). As with graphs, tables should be clearly labelled and titled.

Table 7.2 An example of a table

The average number of aggressive acts a week in children attending different hours of day care	
Number of hours' day care a week	Average number of aggressive acts per week
0–5	1
6–10	3
11–15	2
16–20	4
21–25	2
26–30	3
31–35	9

Measures of central tendency

Measures of central tendency display the 'mid-point' values of sets of data.

- The *mean* is calculated by totalling scores and dividing by the number of scores. For example: $1 + 1 + 2 + 3 + 4 + 5 + 6 + 7 + 8 = 37$; $37/9 = 4.2$. Its strengths are that it is the most accurate measure of central tendency and includes all scores. Its weaknesses are that it is skewed by extreme scores and the mean score may not actually be one of the scores.
- The *median* is the central value of scores in rank order. For example: for the set of data 1, 1, 2, 3, 4, 5, 6, 7, 8 – the median is 4. With an odd number of scores this is the middle number, while with an even number of scores it is the average of the 2 middle scores. Its strengths are that it is not affected by extreme scores and is easier to calculate than the mean. Its weaknesses are that it lacks the sensitivity of the mean and can be unrepresentative in a small set of data.
- The *mode* is the most common value. For example: for the set of data 2, 3, 6, 7, 7, 7, 9, 15, 16, 16, 20 – the mode is 7. Its strengths are that it is less affected by extreme scores and, unlike the mean, is always a whole number. Its weaknesses are that there can be more than one mode and it does not use all scores.

MEASURES OF DISPERSION

Measures of dispersion are measures of variability in a set of data.

- The *range* is calculated by subtracting the lowest from the highest value. Its strengths are that it is easy to calculate and includes extreme values, while its weaknesses are that it is distorted by extreme scores and does not indicate if data are clustered or spread evenly around the mean.
- The *interquartile range* displays the variability of the middle 50 per cent of a set of data. Its strengths are that it is easy to calculate and is not affected by extreme scores, while its weaknesses are that it does not include all scores and is inaccurate if there are big intervals between scores.
- *Standard deviation* measures the variability (spread) of a set of scores from the mean. Its strengths are that it is more sensitive than the range, as all values are included and it allows the interpretation of individual values, while its weaknesses are that it is more complex to calculate and is less meaningful if data are not normally distributed.

Normal distribution

Normal distribution occurs when data have an even amount of scores either side of the mean. Normally distributed data are symmetrical – when such data are plotted on a graph they form a bell-shaped curve with as many scores below the mean as above. (See also **page 68**.)

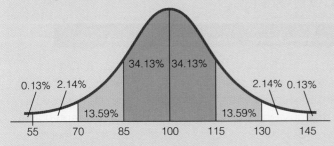

Fig 7.10 Normal distribution of IQ scores

Checking data for normal distribution

- *Examine visually* – inspect the data to see if scores are mainly around the mean.
- *Calculate measure of central tendency* – work out the mean, median and mode to see if they are similar.
- *Plot the frequency distribution* – put the data into a histogram to see if they form a bell-shaped curve.

SKEWED DISTRIBUTION

If data do not have a symmetrical distribution, the resulting graph is *skewed* and does not have an even amount of scores either side of the norm. *Outliers* ('freak' scores) can cause skewed distributions.

- A *positive* skewed distribution occurs when there is a high extreme score or group of scores.
- A *negative* skewed distribution occurs when there is a low extreme score or group of scores.

So a positively skewed distribution has more high than low scores in it, while a negatively skewed distribution has more low than high scores in it.

Checking data for skewed distribution

The same ways that data are checked for normal distribution are used. Plotting data on a histogram will show if a skew is negative or positive.

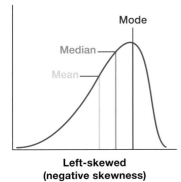

Left-skewed (negative skewness)

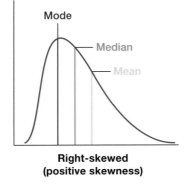

Right-skewed (positive skewness)

Fig 7.11 Skewed distributions

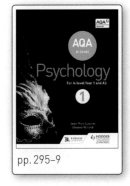

pp. 295–9

7 Research methods

The peer review process and implications of research for the economy

Peer review is essential to scholarly communication and the verification process. It involves the expert scrutiny of research papers to determine scientific validity. Only when perceived as valid may papers be published in respected journals, and therefore peer review is regarded as a 'gatekeeper', lessening the possibility that unscientific research is published and accepted as scientific fact. The process involves several experts being sent a copy of a research paper by a journal editor, with several possible outcomes:

- Accept the work unconditionally
- Accept if modifications are made
- Reject, but suggest revisions
- Reject outright.

❌ Criticisms of peer review

✗ There are many organisations with interests in ensuring that only certain research is published, for example drug companies desiring studies published that suggest their products are effective, and this puts pressure on those involved in peer review to remain independent and unbiased.

✗ Research operates in a narrow social world that makes it difficult to peer review in an objective, unbiased way, due to jealousies, past differences etc. that may occur between researchers.

✗ Reviewers have been accused of not validating research for publication so that their own work may be published first. Indeed, claims are even made of reviewers plagiarising research they were supposed to be scrutinising and passing it off as their own.

✗ Peer review can be slow, sometimes taking years to achieve.

Fig 7.4 Self-selected sampling involves participants volunteering to take part in a study

The implications of psychological research for the economy

Psychological research continually leads to practical applications that benefit people's lives, which in turn benefits the economy. This is especially true for mental health. Ten per cent of people will spend time in a mental institution during their lifetime and 1 in 3 people will receive treatment for mental problems. Therefore, effective treatments, developed from psychological research, make huge savings in financial terms by enabling people to return to work and contribute more fully to the economy through the wages they earn and spend and through the increased taxes that they contribute. Effective strategies to deal with mental health also reduce the long-term financial costs on the health service from having to deal with people who would have remained ill without such treatments.

RESEARCH

- Koran *et al.* (2000) gave an additional treatment of the antipsychotic drug olanzapine to a group of OCD sufferers who had not responded to a course of treatment with the antidepressant drug fluoxetine, while treatment with the antidepressant continued. It was found that the combined treatment produced improvements in reducing OCD symptoms. This suggests that a combined drug therapy is useful in addressing treatment-resistant forms of OCD, thus benefiting the economy by getting people back to work and reducing the burden on the health services.

- Brosnan & Thorpe (2006) gave a group of participants who had a fear of using computers a 10-week course of systematic desensitisation (SD) and found that their fear levels became comparable to a control group of non-fearful participants. A second group of similarly treated participants were compared to a non-treated group of participants with a fear of using computers and were followed up for a year. Fear levels were significantly lowered in the fearful group, which suggests that SD is an effective treatment for reducing technophobia and therefore allows such people to work and contribute to the economy.

✔ Evaluation

✔ As well as producing a better functioning workforce and reducing costs to the health service, psychological research also cuts costs in policing, the judiciary, the prison services etc., as psychologically healthy people are less likely to incur costs on these institutions.

✔ When conducting research, psychologists need to remember that ethical considerations come before profit and that psychology should not be used to exploit people, for instance by producing practical applications that have negative consequences, like manipulating social influences to get people to conform and carry out immoral practices in the workplace.

✔ In conducting research and producing practical applications, psychologists must ensure that they do not become divorced from the consequences of their actions. An example might be conducting research into psychoactive drugs, the results of which are then misused by drug companies to produce treatments that increase the companies' profits but have negative consequences for the people who use the drugs.

pp. 279–80

8 Revision and exam skills
Revision

When first practising exam questions you will need all learning materials to hand, such as notes and handouts. Ensure you fully understand the requirements of the question from the *command words* and know how much to write by referring to the number of *marks* on offer. Make a plan in numbered or bullet point form, and then have a go at writing your answer, giving yourself the same amount of time as in the real exam (about 1 minute and 15 seconds per mark). You will probably have to refer to learning materials when writing your answer, but as you become familiar with this method, you will increasingly be able to write answers without them. A good way to achieve this is to read through relevant materials first, then put them away before writing your answer.

Revision strategies

Many students incorrectly see revision as something done immediately before examinations. Although pre-examination revision is important, revision is something that you should incorporate into your studies regularly throughout the course and indeed is an integral part of the learning process. At the end of studying each element of a topic, revise the material to develop a deeper understanding and to check that you have covered everything and that you fully understand it. The best way to achieve this is to engage with the material, for example by reading through notes/worksheets etc. and highlighting the main points. Make use of available textbooks to further elaborate your

All topics need to be revised, including ones you find difficult, as they have an equal chance of being on the exam paper. Ensure you have listed all the topics on the specification and have all materials necessary for revising each topic. Find somewhere comfortable to revise away from distractions. Make sure that everything you need for revising, like tidying up your desk, is done before revision starts. It is easy to spend all the designated revision time on distraction activities, like sorting out books and sharpening pencils. About 90 minutes a session will be best, using the revision method you have practised all year – namely, reading through necessary materials, highlighting important points, using previous exam questions to construct answers. Give yourself a planned reward for completing revision sessions, be it chocolate or a favourite TV programme. Revising in a constant, organised way like this is the best route to maximising exam performance.

knowledge; better candidates will be making use of more than just one source of information. After this, attempt an exam-type question to assess your level of knowledge and understanding and also to familiarise yourself with the kind of questions you may be asked in the exam. Such questions can be accessed on the AQA website, where you will find sample questions. These also include (in the mark schemes) advice on what types of things to include in your answer. Over time, make sure that you include all types of possible questions in your revision, not just those concerning outlining and describing, but also those requiring explanations and evaluations.

MAKING A REVISION TIMETABLE

Before starting pre-exam revision you will need a revision timetable. This is best achieved by having morning, afternoon and evening sessions for each day (though there is no reason why you can't divide your days up differently, for example just morning and afternoon sessions, or even hour by hour). You can then use this as a template for each separate week of revision.

For each of your subjects, make a list of the topics you need to revise. Then, using a pencil at first, slot in the topics, making sure that you first block out any sessions that are not available due to other commitments. It is probably best initially to revise subjects and topics that will be examined first. A revision programme has to be achievable, so ensure that there are a few spare slots each week to use if any planned revision sessions do not occur. When you have finally got all the topics entered, colour them in using a different colour for each subject.

Put your revision timetable up on a wall and tick off sessions as you go. You might even give a copy to a parent so they can police you and make sure sessions get done. Having a revision timetable like this increases confidence that revision can be completed, which in turn increases motivation to revise.

Time	Monday	Tuesday	Wednesday	Thursday	Friday	Saturday	Sunday
9am–11am	Social influence		Memory			Attachment	
11am–1pm	BREAK	BREAK	BREAK	BREAK	BREAK	BREAK	BREAK
1pm–3pm		Psychopathology			Research methods		
3pm–5pm	BREAK	BREAK	BREAK	BREAK	BREAK	BREAK	BREAK
5pm–7pm				Approaches			Biopsychology
7pm–9pm		Research methods					

Fig 8.1 Revision timetable

8 Revision and exam skills
Exam skills

The exams

For the AS qualification, students sit two papers:

- **Paper 1** is called 'Introductory topics' and consists of three sections: the social psychology topic of *social influence,* the cognitive psychology topic of *memory* and the developmental psychology topic of *attachment.* Each of these sections is worth 24 marks, for a total of 72 marks. Research methods questions will be incorporated into all three of these sections. Paper 1 accounts for 50 per cent of the overall marks for the AS. You will have 90 minutes to sit this paper, with all questions being compulsory for all candidates.
- **Paper 2** is called 'Psychology in context' and again consists of three sections: *approaches*, the individual differences topic of *psychopathology* and lastly *research methods*. Each of these sections is worth 24 marks, for a total of 72 marks (and thus an overall total for both papers of 144 marks). Research methods questions can again occur in all sections. Paper 2 accounts for 50 per cent of the overall marks for the AS. You will have 90 minutes to sit this paper, with all questions being compulsory for all candidates.

TYPES OF MARKS

There are three types of marks that can be gained in the examination.

- **AO1 marks** These marks are awarded for relevant *description* of psychological knowledge – for example, describing the multi-store model of memory. The availability of these marks in a question can be identified by the use of certain *exam injunctions* ('command words' – the words in a question that inform you what kind of answer is required) within the question (see below for a list and explanation of exam injunctions).
- **AO2 marks** These marks are awarded for relevant *application* of psychological knowledge to scenarios that are provided – for example, applying your knowledge of normative social influence to a scenario that illustrates its usage. The availability of these marks in a question can again be identified by the use of certain *exam injunctions*.
- **AO3 marks** These marks are awarded for relevant *evaluation* of psychological knowledge – for example, assessing the degree of research support for the learning theory explanation of attachment formation. The availability of these marks in a question can once again be identified by the use of certain *exam injunctions*.

The exam process

You may have attended all your lessons, completed all your work, revised hard and be extremely motivated to succeed. However, unless you perform well in your examinations you will not get what you deserve. Therefore, it is essential that you fully understand the exam process in order to fully achieve and get that grade you want.

Exam injunctions are the 'command words' in a question, the words that tell you what kind of an answer is required in terms of description, application and evaluation. Some questions may involve creating answers that focus on only one of these injunctions, for example a 'description only' answer, while other questions may involve creating answers that focus on two exam injunctions, for example a 'description and evaluation' question. There is even the possibility of an 'application essay', which would require creating an answer that focused on all three of the injunctions.

In order to fully understand what type of answer you should be writing, familiarise yourself with the following different exam injunctions. This should help you to not fall into the trap of writing answers that contain irrelevant material in terms of what a question requires.

AO1 injunctions
- *Identify* means simply to name, no other description is required
- *Define* involves explaining what is meant by
- *Outline* means give brief details without explanation
- *Describe* means give a detailed account without explanation
- *Correctly complete* means fill in the missing information
- *Select* means choose the correct option

AO2 injunctions
- *Refer* means include information from a certain source

AO3 injunctions
- *Give* means show awareness of
- *Explain* means give a clear account of why and how something is so
- *Evaluate* means assess the value or effectiveness of
- *Discuss* means give a reasoned balanced account (including descriptive and evaluative material)
- *Assess* means judge the quality/importance of

Different question types

There are, broadly speaking, six main types of question. Make sure that you have had regular experience, under exam conditions, of each of them. Remember that all topics can be examined by each of the question types, so ideally you should have familiarity of all question types for all the topics listed in the specification.

Each question type is quite different from other question types and has a certain way in which it must be answered to maximise the number of marks gained. Therefore, it is worthwhile having a look at some common mistakes that students make with each question type and learning some strategies that will help to increase the marks you gain in the actual examination. The differences between one grade and another in the examination can be just a few marks, so by learning and practising strategies that maximise your marks you could very easily improve by one or two grades.

Let's now, on the following pages, have a look at the question types. Sample question answers are on **pages 101, 103, 105, 107, 109 and 111**.

8 Revision and exam skills
Question practice: selection questions

With this type of question you are given information from which you select appropriate choices. There will often be a spare option left over at the end. This is so that a choice always has to be made between options when answering the question.

Question
Match the following descriptions to the types of LTM listed in the table below. One description will be left over.   [3 marks]

A   Knowing that a telephone is for communicating with people

B   Knowing how to ice-skate properly

C   Being able to recall someone's phone number you've just been given by repeating it sub-vocally

D   Knowing that your sister is younger than you

Type of LTM	Description
Semantic	
Episodic	
Procedural	

Strategies for improvement
✔ Ensure you have regular experience of this question type.

✔ Attempt selection questions for all topic areas.

✔ Create your own selection questions, swap them with other students and then mark their answers.

✔ Identify the command words (the words that inform what specific information/skill is required) in questions before attempting them. First, though, you will need to understand what the command words used in questions mean (see **page 99**).

✔ Use the marks in brackets that appear after a question, as an indication of how many selections are required.

Common pitfalls
✗ Unfamiliarity with such questions

✗ Not understanding the requirements of the question

✗ Not making sufficient selections

Answer

Type of LTM	Description
Semantic	*A*
Episodic	*C*
Procedural	*B*

Feedback
2/3 marks. 1 mark for selecting statement A as being an example of semantic memory and 1 mark for selecting statement B as an example of procedural memory, but 0 marks for selecting statement C as an example of episodic memory – the correct selection there would be statement D.

8 Revision and exam skills
Question practice: short-answer questions

This type of question generally requires very specific brief answers, with a need for elaboration (detail) to gain any additional marks available.

Short-answer questions can require description-only type answers (AO1), like this Question 1, taken from the psychopathology topic.

Such questions can also require evaluation-only type answers (AO3), like this Question 2, again taken from the psychopathology topic.

Questions

1 Outline the deviation from social norms definition of abnormality.   [3 marks]
2 Explain one strength of the deviation from social norms definition of abnormality. [2 marks]

Strategies for improvement

✔ Identify the command words before attempting the question (as with selection questions).

✔ Use the marks in brackets as a guide as to how much to write. In an exam you would have about 1 minute 15 seconds per mark available, so a 2-mark short-answer question should take you about 2 minutes 30 seconds to answer, while a 3-mark question should take about 3 minutes 45 seconds. As the average student writes about 25 words a minute, then that works out at 50 words for a 2-mark question and 75 words for a 3-mark question.

✔ Use the partial mark technique. This can be used for short-answer questions worth up to 3 marks, as such questions are assessed by examiners referring to mark descriptors, which guide examiners as to what an answer should contain to earn different amounts of marks.

So if, for example, a question is worth 3 marks, create an answer worth 1 mark and then add sufficient elaboration (detail) to earn 2 marks and then again to create an answer worth 3 marks. So for the question 'Outline the failure to function adequately definition of abnormality. [3 marks]', first produce an answer worth 1 mark, such as '**The failure to function adequately definition sees abnormality as an inability to cope with day-to-day living**'. Then add to this sufficient elaboration to gain the second available mark, such as '**The failure to function adequately definition sees abnormality as an inability to cope with day-to-day living, *such as by disrupting the ability to work and conduct everyday relationships*'**. Then finally add further elaboration to gain access to the third mark available, such as '**The failure to function adequately definition sees abnormality as an inability to cope with day-to-day living, *such as by disrupting the ability to work and conduct everyday relationships. Such individuals often cannot experience the range of emotions and behaviours that others can*'**.

✔ Create examples for all topics on the specification. You could even match up with another student and answer and mark each other's efforts.

✔ Practise short-answer questions regularly under exam-type conditions.

Answer 1

The definition sees abnormality as behaviour that violates social rules, such as by being naked in public.

Feedback
2/3 marks. 1 mark is earned for stating the definition sees abnormality as behaviour violating social rules, with the example that follows being sufficient elaboration to earn an additional mark. Additional elaboration would be needed to gain the third mark, such as by explaining 'that social norms are unwritten rules for acceptable behaviour'.

Exam tip
1 mark would be earned for a relevant point, with up to 2 further marks for sufficient elaboration (detail).

Answer 2

One strength of the definition would be that it helps protect society.

Feedback
1/2 marks. A relevant strength is identified, so 1 mark is gained, but no more than that as there is no elaboration which shows understanding of the point being made, such as that the definition helps protect society by allowing the state to intervene in abnormal people's lives.

Exam tip
1 mark would be earned for a relevant point, with an additional mark available for sufficient elaboration.

Question practice: application questions

With this type of question, your answer needs to combine relevant psychological knowledge with information drawn from a given scenario. Common problems include giving the correct psychological knowledge but not linking it to the scenario, commenting about the scenario but without linking it to relevant psychological knowledge, and not writing sufficient information to gain access to all the marks available.

The key to correctly answering this type of question is to provide the necessary psychological knowledge, in this instance explain what unanimity is and the effect it can have upon conformity levels, while simultaneously using information drawn from the scenario as evidence to support the explanation. Generally speaking, if you provide only psychological knowledge (however good the description is) and you include no application to the scenario, then only half marks can be awarded. (The same is true of an essay that is all application and no description of relevant knowledge.)

Question
When a group of Trevor's friends said they all thought that the tea in the college cafeteria tasted like coffee, Trevor found himself publicly agreeing with them, even though privately he thought it did taste like tea. However, a few days later when his friends all agreed again that the tea tasted like coffee, but one friend stated that she thought it tasted like drinking chocolate, Trevor felt able to truthfully state that it tasted like tea.

Refer to the scenario above to explain how unanimity affects conformity rates.   [4 marks]

Strategies for improvement
✔ Use the marks in brackets at the end of the question as an indication of how much to write (as with short-answer questions).

✔ Use the PEA rule: (P) make a critical **p**oint, (E) **e**xplain it, (A) **a**pply it.

✔ Use two highlighter pens – one colour to highlight psychological knowledge and another colour to highlight the application in your answer. This way you can easily see if you are getting the 'balance' right between the amount of psychological knowledge and application to the scenario.

✔ Practise such answers in pairs; one of you does the theory part, the other one does the application part.

✔ Regularly practise strategies that get you to apply your psychological knowledge to a specific scenario until it becomes an automatic process to do so.

✔ Make sure you have attempted application type questions for all topic areas.

Answer

Unanimity concerns how much agreement there is within a majority group. The greater the level of agreement, then the more likely it is that an individual would conform. In a variation of Asch's experiment, one dissenter gave the correct answer when the rest of the confederates all gave the same wrong answer and conformity fell from the 32 per cent that occurred when all confederates gave the wrong answer to just 5.5 per cent. Indeed, when a dissenter gave a different wrong answer, conformity still fell sharply to 9 per cent. This shows that dissenters model that disagreement with a majority is possible.

Feedback

2/4 marks. A really good, informative and coherent explanation of what unanimity is and how a lack of it reduces conformity. It is well backed up with relevant research evidence, too. Unfortunately, as too many students do with this type of question, there is no engagement with the scenario. The candidate here could easily have talked about how Trevor felt pressured to conform when all his friends said the tea tasted like coffee, but less pressured when a dissenter gave a different answer to the majority, even though their opinion was different again to Trevor's.

Exam tip

However good the quality of the psychological knowledge concerning how unanimity affects conformity rates is, no more than 2 marks will be earned unless there is sufficient reference to the scenario to back up the points made.

8 Revision and exam skills
Question practice: research methods questions

This type of question requires answers centred on aspects of research methods, often focused on questions formed around specific topic areas. Sometimes such questions are orientated at a general research methods topic area, for example, Question 1.

Such questions therefore only require you to focus on the general topic area specified, in this case the strengths of a repeated measures design. However, this type of question can also be more specific in its requirements, for example Question 2.

Research methods questions can often involve mathematical skills. They may require calculations, such as in Question 3, drawn from the memory topic.

Such questions can also merely require knowledge of mathematical skills to be exhibited, such as in Question 4.

Questions

1   [After description of a research study] The study uses a repeated measures design. Explain one strength of the repeated measures design.   [2 marks]

2   A researcher tested the effect of sleep deprivation by getting two groups of participants, one who had eight hours' sleep last night and one who had none, to do an IQ test. One group of participants did the test in one room while the other group did it in a different room.

    Identify a possible extraneous variable in the above study and explain what its effect could be on the findings if it was uncontrolled.   [3 marks]

3   A group of female participants and a group of male participants read some information about the meanings of various words and one week later were given a test of recall to assess their semantic LTM ability.

    The scores gained in the test can be seen below. Calculate the mean score for semantic LTM for male participants. Show your calculations.   [2 marks]

Participant	Male scores on test of semantic LTM (out of 20)	Female scores on test of semantic LTM (out of 20)
1	10	11
2	11	10
3	14	16
4	8	9
5	16	15
6	8	9
7	12	11
8	9	11

4   What type of graph should be used to plot data from a correlational analysis?   [1 mark]

Strategies for improvement

✔ Identify command words before attempting an answer.

✔ Use marks in brackets as a guide to how much to write/how much elaboration is required.

✔ Practise these types of questions for all topic areas regularly.

✔ Use the partial answer technique (see **page 102**).

Answer 1

One strength of a repeated measures design is that there are no participant variables.

Feedback

1/2 marks. Correct, but no elaboration of the point, so only 1 mark. The candidate could have gone on to explain why there are no participant variables, for example because each participant is compared against themselves.

Answer 2

One extraneous variable could be the fact that the participants did the test in different rooms. This could make the results invalid.

Feedback

2/3 marks. 1 mark for correct identification of a possible extraneous variable and 1 additional mark for the comments on the validity of the results. Elaboration would be required to gain the other mark, possibly by explaining how the extraneous variable could become a confounding one.

Answer 3

The mean is 11.

Working out:

$10 + 11 + 14 + 8 + 16 + 8 + 12 + 9 = 88$

88 divided by 8 = 11

Feedback

2/2 marks. Correct, and the calculations are shown, so full marks.

Answer 4

A scattergram would be used.

Feedback

1/1 mark. Correct.

Exam tips

Answer 1: 1 mark would be earned by making a relevant point, with an additional mark available for sufficient elaboration.

Answer 2: To gain the first mark on offer an extraneous variable needs to be identified, but this must be drawn from the scenario. The other 2 marks would be for explaining its possible effect in confounding the results. Sufficient elaboration would be necessary to get the second mark.

Answer 3: 1 mark for correct calculation of the mean, with an additional mark for showing the calculations to achieve this

Answer 4: 1 mark for each correct identification of a scattergram (or scattergraph)

Question practice: research study questions

This type of question requires answers that focus on description and/or evaluation of research studies. Descriptive content will need to focus on aims, procedure and conclusions of research studies, while evaluation could centre on methodological and ethical considerations, as well as what conclusions can be drawn, for example the degree of support for an explanation. There are some studies that are explicitly listed in the specification, such as Pavlov's research into classical conditioning, so these could form the basis of such questions, for example Question 1, which is drawn from the approaches topic. Questions could also be asked that allow a choice of research study, for example Question 2.

Questions

1   Outline Pavlov's research into classical conditioning.   [6 marks]
2   Outline and evaluate one research study of the biological treatment of OCD.   [6 marks]

Strategies for improvement

✔   Identify command words before attempting an answer.

✔   Use marks in brackets as a guide to how much to write/how much elaboration is required.

✔   Make sure you have studied a research study in sufficient detail (aims, procedure, findings, conclusions and evaluative points) for all topic areas.

✔   Make sure you have studied in sufficient detail all studies that are explicitly listed in the specification.

✔   Practise these types of questions for all topic areas regularly.

Common pitfalls

✘   Providing too little necessary detail

✘   Focusing on the wrong elements of a study (for example, giving findings and conclusions when the question explicitly asks for the aims and procedure)

✘   Using studies solely as a form of evaluation rather than describing the necessary features

Answer 1

Pavlov was the pioneer researcher into classical conditioning. He became interested while researching into the role of salivation in digestion in dogs, as to how dogs learned through association to predict the arrival of their food. Using the reflex action of salivation, Pavlov found that if a bell was rung seven times when food was presented to a dog it would subsequently salivate just to the bell. Originally the dog would only have salivated to the presentation of food. It was concluded that the dog had learned to associate the sound of the bell to being fed, hence the salivation in anticipation of food.

Feedback

4/6 marks. A 'solid' description of Pavlov's research is evident. It is accurate, relevant and coherent. However, there is a lack of detail and specialist terminology, which prevents the answer being placed in the top level of marks. This could have been achieved by using specialist terms like 'unconditioned stimulus', 'conditioned stimulus' and 'conditioned response' when describing Pavlov's research to show a higher level of detail and understanding.

Exam tip

Marks would only be awarded for description of Pavlov's research, so any evaluation would not earn credit and would waste valuable time. The actual mark gained would depend on the level of accurate detail provided.

Answer 2

One research study into the effectiveness of anti-depressants in treating OCD was a study by Koran et al. (2000). They aimed to see how effective olanzapine was when combined with the SRI drug fluoxetine in treating non-responsive forms of OCD. There were 10 participants, all of whom had had OCD for at least a year. They were being treated with fluoxetine and increased levels of olanzapine were then added to their treatment for 8 weeks. The findings showed that the combined treatment was superior in reducing symptoms than by treatments with just fluoxetine alone. Some participants did suffer the side-effect of significant weight increase.

Feedback

4/6 marks. A good answer in terms of description – there is accurate and somewhat detailed reference to the aim, procedure and findings of the study. However, the answer is very unbalanced, as only the final sentence can be classed as evaluation.

Exam tip

The answer calls for both description and evaluation of a relevant research study. Description could be achieved by detailing the aims, procedure and findings. The evaluation could focus on relevant methodological and ethical points, as well as what conclusions could be drawn about the effectiveness of the treatment.

8 Revision and exam skills
Question practice: essays and longer-answer questions

This type of question will generally require both descriptive and evaluative material (but could be just description or evaluation), with a maximum of 12 marks at AS. Such questions can include application essays requiring description and/or evaluation with, additionally, use of information drawn from a scenario provided.

Questions

1 Discuss minority influence.   [12 marks]

2 'Sometimes I agree with the majority so that I will "fit in" and be accepted,' said Janet. 'I often agree with the majority too', said Susan, 'but usually when I'm in a new situation where I don't know how to behave.'

   Discuss two explanations of majority influence. As part of your discussion, refer to the comments expressed by Janet and Susan.   [12 marks]

Strategies for improvement

✔ Identify command words before starting an answer.

✔ Practise writing to the mark allocation – remember it is about 1 minute 15 seconds per mark (that is 7½ minutes of description and 7½ minutes of evaluation in a 12-mark question) or alternatively about 20 words per minute.

✔ Structure answers so that they have a common 'theme' running through them.

✔ Shape material to specifically meet the requirements of a question.

✔ Only use methodological material where it specifically fits the needs of a question.

✔ Practise dividing answers up into separate paragraphs.

✔ Create (and practise using) lists of specialist terms that go with each topic area.

✔ Practise building your evaluative material into elaborated commentaries that use several types of evaluation built upon each other.

✔ Shape material as evaluation by signalling its usage as such – for example, by using phrases such as 'research support comes from …' and 'these findings suggest that …'.

✔ Practise assessments under exam conditions regularly.

Common pitfalls

✘ Failure to address command words

✘ Not writing to the mark allocation – often by producing too much description

✘ Wandering off the question

✘ Irrelevant use of methodological points

✘ Lack of organisation into paragraphs

✘ Lack of specialist terminology

✘ Lack of elaboration/commentary

✘ Not 'shaping' material as evaluation – material intended as evaluation can often be phrased as descriptive material

✘ Use of generic content (material that is not specifically focused on the question)

Answer 1

Minority influence is a type of social influence that motivates individuals to reject established majority group norms and become converted to acceptance of the minority group's attitudes and behaviour. This generally occurs through informational social influence, where a minority provides new ideas and information to the majority.

One important factor in minority influence is consistency, with a minority being more persuasive the more consistent they are in their attitudes and behaviour, as it shows their commitment to their beliefs. Moscovici (1969) found that consistent minorities were more persuasive in getting participants to agree wrongly that blue slides were actually green than inconsistent minorities were.

Another important factor is flexibility. Minorities who show some flexibility in their stance, demonstrate their ability to be moderate, co-operative and reasonable, and this makes them even more persuasive than consistent minorities, who are seen to some extent to be rigid and uncompromising. Nemeth (1968) found that a minority who showed some flexibility in arguing for a much lower rate of compensation to a victim of an accident than a majority group, had more influence in changing the majority's viewpoint than a similar minority that showed no flexibility. This suggests that flexibility is a more influential factor than that of consistency.

There are other factors too that can affect the persuasiveness of a minority group. One of these is style of thinking. Minorities who are successful in converting people to their viewpoint, do so because they get them to indulge in systematic processing where the minority viewpoint is considered carefully over time, resulting in a change in people's belief systems.

Minority influence can be seen as a form of internalisation, also known as true conformity, because it involves a fundamental change in people's belief systems, which leads to a very strong form of conformity to the minority's viewpoint, which is maintained outside of their presence.

Feedback

9/12 marks. A good level of knowledge and understanding of minority influence is demonstrated, with a commendable amount of accurate detail contained within the description – for example, the degree of influence that the factors of consistency, flexibility and systematic processing have in converting people's belief. There is also creditworthy descriptive material concerning the link to internalisation. There is some decent evaluation, but probably not enough of it to allow the answer to be placed in the highest mark level. Two research studies are used and both fairly effectively, though the Moscovici study lacks some important detail. The Nemeth study is better, as it is used to illustrate that flexibility is more influential than consistency in bringing about conversion to a minority viewpoint. The quality of the answer could be improved by provision of more research evidence, or maybe by highlighting the important role of minority influence in bringing about social change.

Exam tip

6 marks are available here for a description of minority influence, which could be achieved by detailing the factors associated with it. A further 6 marks are available for evaluation, which could be achieved by detailing what research evidence suggests about minority influence.

Answer 2

One explanation for social influence is that of normative social influence, which occurs when individuals want to be accepted or to avoid rejection by a majority. This involves compliance, a weak form of conformity that only involves public, but not private, acceptance of the majority's viewpoint. It is additionally a weak form of conformity, as it is only temporary, not being maintained outside the presence of the majority group. An example of informational social influence would be someone who dresses in a certain style of clothing to fit in at a party, even though they don't really like that style of clothing.

This is demonstrated by Janet, who admits that she conforms to majority viewpoints merely to be accepted and fit in. This form of social influence was supported by Asch (1956) who found he could get participants to agree to obviously wrong answers given by a majority group.

Another explanation of majority influence is that of informational social influence, which occurs when individuals are in an ambiguous situation that gives no clear indication of what the right answer or behaviour would be. They therefore look to the majority for information as to how they should act. This especially occurs when the majority is seen as being more experienced or knowledgeable. For example, if someone was in a restaurant for the first time and didn't know which cutlery, glasses and so forth to use, then they might look to other more experienced diners for guidance as to which they should use. It can be argued that informational social influence involves internalisation, as individuals become convinced of the validity of the opinions and behaviour exhibited by the majority.

Susan shows informational social influence, as she admits she conforms when she's in a new situation and doesn't know how to behave. Informational social influence was highlighted by Jenness (1932), who showed that estimates of sweets in a jar moved towards a group estimate.

Feedback

9/12 marks. Two relevant explanations are identified and clearly described, with good evidence of accurate detail and the provision of examples that demonstrate the candidate's understanding of the explanations, as well as correctly linking the explanations to types of conformity. The application of the provided scenario is done accurately and coherently in a way that again shows the candidate's understanding of the explanation. The Asch and Jenness studies are used as evaluation, but in both instances there is a need to 'shape' the findings more effectively so that they illustrate how normative and informational social influence are occurring.

Exam tip

6 marks would be available here for description of two explanations of social influence, with 4 marks available for their evaluation, probably most easily achieved by detailing research that highlights how they operate, and a final 2 marks for application of the scenario to the answer.